The Miracle

The Miracle

A Memoir

by
James M. LeBlanc

XULON PRESS

Xulon Press
2301 Lucien Way #415
Maitland, FL 32751
407.339.4217
www.xulonpress.com

Unless otherwise indicated, Scripture quotations taken from the King James Version (KJV)–*public domain.*

Printed in the United States of America.

ISBN-13: 978-1-6312-9711-3
Ebook: 978-1-6312-9712-0

Dedication

The Miracle is dedicated to my lovely bride, Marchelle. Thank you honey, I love you.

Table of Contents

Chapter 1

In the Beginning

Laying on the top bunk in the dormitory-style prison block in Moshannon Valley Correctional Facility in Philipsburg, Pennsylvania, I folded my hands behind my head and listened to the constant scraping. It was late at night; the lights were out and the only noise to be heard was "scrape-scrape-scrape..." I knew this sound was produced by the Washington DC inmates I was housed with who were taking shifts in the bathroom sharpening shanks in preparation for the upcoming war with the Latinos. This could not be my reality. How did I, a kid from Berkeley, California end up in the mountains of Pennsylvania preparing for a prison riot at the age of 38? As I lay in fearful sleeplessness, I thought back to the journey that brought me there.

San Francisco, California was a continental divide away from the mountains of Western Pennsylvania, yet it is where my life began on February 15, 1969. I was born on that day and it was not until I was 48 years old that I would learn that I was actually conceived in Washington DC, where my biological parents met. My daddy was black, and my mom was white. He was married but not to her. My mom didn't find this out until she told him she was pregnant, and he informed her, in no uncertain terms, that he was married. She left and went back to California with me in her womb and my three-year-old brother in tow. My mom then made a tough decision. Figuring I would have a better chance with a more established family, she placed me for adoption shortly after my birth. For all intent and purposes, I was born an orphan.

The good news was that I was adopted immediately. My parents, a white couple from Berkeley, CA. had already adopted two white children before me: my sister, Barbara and my brother, Christopher. This was in the 1960's. America was changing, and to a young, liberal white couple in Berkeley, racism was a thing that was fading away and would probably be totally eradicated by the time their brown baby boy grew up. They had the best intentions and they did give me a life with advantages that would serve me well; however, the emotional baggage that came with these circumstances along with a genetic predisposition to addiction almost proved fatal.

Berkeley, Ca. in the 1970's was a fantastic place to grow up. Full of parks, playgrounds, and endless adventures, a young boy couldn't have asked for more. Then there was a diverse mix of liberal academia who emerged from the University of California, (Cal), and mostly lived in the hills. The working class, of all races, lived in the flatlands. The Cal students were sprinkled throughout, and the hippies who emerged from the 60's lived pretty much anywhere they dang well pleased. Right next door and to the south of Berkeley is Oakland; one of the toughest cities in America and directly north of Berkeley is Richmond, another notorious city. Cocooned in the middle of these rough spots sits Berkeley, otherwise known as "Bezerkely" or "B-Town" as we affectionately called our hometown back in the day.

We called home a house in the hills. Greenwood Terrace was, (and is) about as picturesque a neighborhood as you could get. Not wealthy by a long shot; my mom and dad received an inheritance in the early 1960's that they spent on a house in the hills, allowing them to move out of their tiny apartment in the flatlands. They only had one child at the time, my sister, Barbara. Chris and I were brought into the fold after the move.

Our home was a beautiful house designed by Bernard Maybeck, a famous Bay Area architect during the first half of the 20th century. It had a very rough basement, two floors and an attic which was actually livable as my sister proved during her teenage years There was a brick walkway leading up to the front door. A nice front lawn and garden were set off by a huge redwood tree which grew between the side of the front lawn and the street. We had a driveway long enough for two cars, with a tree that we used to climb with a branch that hung over the driveway. We climbed that tree often until my sister fell off that hanging branch one day and landed smack on her rear-end on the hood of our trusty Volvo station wagon. There was a small sitting area on the front patio where I often was forced to sit and think of a reason why my mother should let me in when I arrived home after curfew.

When you walked in our front door there was a small foyer that split off: three stairs down to the main level and 12 steps to the upper level. These were divided by staircases of three, seven and two. This was important because I considered myself a big boy when I could jump down the seven-step staircase in one bound without injury. There was a heavy, wooden sliding door that, when used, separated the two levels. That was because the house was originally built to be a duplex and both levels could be fully functional, separate habitats. Downstairs was a large, open living room with an alcove on one end and a fireplace on the other. There were four large picture windows with two of them affording an amazing view of the San Francisco Bay and The City across the Bay. This view was obscured over the years by neighbors' trees; however, I remember the amazing lights of San Francisco and the surrounding bay area at night as well as the endless sailboats filling the bay on the weekends.

Off the living room to the right was the kitchen and to the left was the dining room with a bathroom, adjacent off the dining room. This was originally the downstairs bedroom, so the bathroom made more sense in the original configuration. Behind the kitchen was the laundry room and you could continue out the backdoor and down the stone steps to the two-level backyard. The upper level was covered with fir bark and had a sandbox and a swing set, while the lower level was a lawn, plant beds, and a rock garden. My memories of the backyard include weeding that rock garden and mowing the lawn with our old push mower stopping every three minutes to remove the clumped-up grass from the blades which had stopped rotating.

The first seven years of my life were filled with wonderful, good memories. I loved romping in our spacious backyard with my siblings, Charlie the family dog, and our many cats. My mother loved to rescue cats from the Humane Society and we always had between three to five felines living with us which is probably why I love both dogs and cats to this day. The cats were outdoor cats and had their own cat door built into the back door. My favorite was Pandora, a beautiful Siamese who was the matriarch of the brood. I was so enamored with Pandora that I "married" her when I was four years old in a ceremony officiated by my sister Barbara with my brother Chris serving as the witness.

Family outings to the old Ringling Brothers and Barnum and Bailey's three-ring circus were amazing events for me during those early years. Camping trips, excursions to the swimming pool at Strawberry Canyon and Cal Bears' football games were just some of the highlights of my early childhood. I loved rushing the field after the games with all the fans. It always smelled like a mixture of cut grass and sweat and I loved it! The players were impossibly big, and I looked at them as superheroes. We sang the songs with the Cal Band and then followed behind them as they marched through campus after the games. Then our family would walk home where my brother and I would try to destroy each other on the front lawn imitating the players.

The neighborhood playground was called Hillside. Hillside was a primary school and I attended first-third grade there. The best thing about Hillside, however, was the playground. After school and on weekends, it was absolutely filled with kids of all ages. It was an amazing time that was never again duplicated. I think what made the place so special was that the older kids always included the younger ones in all activities. The ages ranged from college-age down to my friends and I, who were 9-10 when we started participating with them. When we played basketball Eddie, the playground leader, would actually "make teams" which meant splitting people up according to age and skill, so I would always have someone on the opposite team who was either the same age or at an equal skill level. The same would be done when we played "touch" football on the concrete field which yielded many a skinned knee and elbow. Epic games of Hide-and-Seek, Ultimate Frisbee, Three-Flies-Up, and Elimination were also on the menu at Hillside. In the summer, my best friend, Daniel and I met at Hillside early before everyone else began to arrive to play Strike-Out, which is basically one-on-one baseball played with a bat, tennis ball, one mitt, and ground rules designating singles, doubles, triples, and home runs. We played all day and into the evening when, as the sun descended, my mom would stand on our deck and yell, Jiiii-iiimmmmm!!!!" and that would be my cue to literally drop everything and run up the hill for dinner. Hillside was an absolutely magical place that, of course, I didn't really appreciate until later in life.

My dad was a high school math teacher and my mom was a housewife/student in those early years. Every morning when my dad went off to work, the four of us would stand at the door and serenade him with a song, "Bye-Bye Daddy/ Bye-Bye Daddy/ Bye-Bye Daddy/ We're sad to see you go!" When I started kindergarten, my mom would meet me at the bus stop after school with Charlie, an awesome poodle/ terrier mix (mutt) who would joyfully bound up to me with this sort of high-step prance that made me feel like the most loved kid alive. The first seven years of my life were full of good memories.

1976 was the year of the Bicentennial. Every year on the Fourth of July, the whole town would caravan down to the Berkeley Marina to watch the fireworks show. If you've never seen a firework display over the San Francisco Bay I feel sorry for you. It was absolutely amazing, and we went every year. 1976 was special though. They really went all out for the celebration of America's 200th birthday. I sat on one of the rocks on the shore and watched the spectacular show with my family, then when it was over, the traffic jam was also epic, and it seemed like it took forever to get out of there. Probably why I like leaving a bit early whenever I'm at a big event to this day.

In 1976, I turned seven, I broke my knee at Hillside, America celebrated the bi-centennial, and my mom and dad got a divorce. We came downstairs one morning all set to watch cartoons, but Mom called us into the kitchen. "Your father left last night. We can no longer live together. It's not you kids' fault, etc, etc." I believe this was when I started wading in the river of denial. I refused to believe it. I turned on my heel and went into the dining room to watch cartoons. My brother and sister remained in the kitchen to talk to Mom, but I couldn't deal with it. Dad leaving was not in the equation and I had absolutely no tools with which to process it.

After a brief custody battle, which Mom won, we settled into our new "normal." Things changed and not for the better. Mom went to work for minimum wage as a secretary in the Linguistics Department at UC Berkeley. It was convenient because through the years she obtained her master's degree and PhD from that department. Sadly, she also started abusing us physically and psychologically. We never knew what would set her off, so we walked on eggshells every day. Being the youngest, I was spared the brunt of it, but we all caught hell. We were slapped, knocked down, demeaned, locked in our rooms, made to stand in a corner and gobble like a turkey, take cold showers, and a whole lot more; but I guess the worst of it was just a negative, tension-filled home. We had very little money and Mom had to go on food stamps for a few years. The crazy part was that we still lived in a nice neighborhood and all of our neighbors were well off while we were really struggling. This was a hard pill to swallow when all the other kids were doing activities like ski-trips, European vacations, Hawaii, etc. Meanwhile, we were going to bed sad and hungry.

During this period, my brother ran away from home all the time. He would either get picked up by the police or just wander back home dirty and hungry. I learned then that running away was an option and even tried it a couple of times, but it wasn't for me! We might not be eating well at home but at least we were eating! He also taught me how to shoplift from stores, fight and cuss. He even went to neighbors' homes asking for food. Eventually Child Protective Services was brought in and, following their investigation, my mother relinquished custody of him. My brother was removed from the home never to return. He was 12 years old and I was 10.

My dad also felt that Chris was too much to handle so my brother went through the foster care system for about a year and then landed with a great family in Fremont, Ca. He lived with them until he graduated from high school and entered the Air Force. He would come visit us every now and again, but never lived with us after that. For me, the message was sinking in that it didn't pay to love or connect to anyone because they were either going to leave you, hurt you or both. I pretty much shut down emotionally after that and my thinking got a little twisted. I would do weird things like go over to my friend's homes and steal their toys. My mom received many a phone call from parents demanding their sons' toys back. I just didn't understand why I couldn't have anything, and they had so much. So, I stole. I have two sons now and I marvel at how easily they ask us for things. Asking was not even an option growing up, at least during the 5-6 years after the divorce. The answer was always "no," and it might be accompanied with a hard slap that made your ears ring.

Through it all, I loved my mom and was always a mama's boy. Some kids have an amazing ability to forgive, especially when things are so unstable. They just want things to be normal. It never was though. There were times when we really struggled and there was no money. Mom was very proud though and never asked for help or handouts. I'll never forget the one time she came to me, tears streaming down her cheeks and asked me for the $5 I had earned mowing lawns. She simply had no money and we needed food. I ran to my room and grabbed the $5 and gave it to her so that she could buy bread, milk and something to make for dinner. True to her word, she gave it back to me on her next payday.

During this time of pure and utter dysfunction, my mom would teach me the value of a strong work-ethic. I loved playing basketball and every year I wanted to play in the YBA (Youth Basketball Association). The fee was around $30, and Mom told me if I earned half, she would put up the other half. I went around the neighborhood asking for odd jobs. Fifty cents here, a dollar there and I earned my part. I remember Mr. Scott. He was my $5.00 man. He had extremely shaky hands and a gravelly voice from years of smoking a pipe. His mind was sharp as a tack though and I could count on him for yard work, but I earned every penny and Mr. Scott had no problem making me work until I got it right. $5.00 was a lot of cash for a 10-year-old in the 70's and I remember the feeling of money earned for a job well done.

I also had a paper route back then delivering "The Berkeley Gazette." It was quite a route, probably three or four miles or so round-trip, and full of hills. Sundays were the worst! I would have to get up before dawn, fold the inserts into the papers, put the papers in their bags, load my paperboy pouch front and back, and struggle to get it on. The papers were so big on Sunday and I was so frail; that I would have to do half my route, walk home, struggle the other half of the papers onto my shoulders, and then walk all the way back to where I had stopped to complete my route. I'll never forget the smell of paper and ink coming from those stacks of newspaper as they sat on our porch in the predawn darkness, not a good memory!

Another way I earned money was by 'stringing up' games. During the video arcade craze of the early 80's, we discovered that you could tape thread to a quarter, drop it down the coin slot, find the switch that gives the game credits, and keep fishing up and down to "string up" the limit the game had- usually 99 credits! You could then sell the games off. For example, you could sell ten games for a dollar. There were only a couple of us who had this skill and you were considered a master if you could string up the limit **and** get your quarter back up through the coin slot. I got caught once by Mike, the Korean owner of the Cheshire Cat, which was the restaurant/bar I was hustling out of to earn extra money. He held me in the stockroom until my mom came to get me. We were all scared of Mike. He would sometimes see me playing a game, stalk over to me, and without a word, slap the game violently making it tilt and lose all the credits I had stolen. He wouldn't even check to see if I had gotten them legitimately! (of course I hadn't); he just dispersed justice quickly and with finality! The ironic thing about Mike was that in the midst of all of this, I tutored his uncle, an older guy who spoke **very** limited English. For some reason he asked me to help him with his reading so I started going down to the Cheshire Cat about an hour before the rest of the gang showed up and we would sit at one of the picnic tables in the courtyard outside and read out loud. I'll never forget his halting, accented English, and how sincere he was in his efforts. I corrected him along the way, and after about 45 minutes, we would finish up and he would give me $5.00. Looking back, I'm sure he saw that I was a smart kid with a good spirit, and he thought this would keep me from committing my petty larceny in his shop. Quite the contrary, it did not. I considered it bonus money. This was the recurring theme in the story of the first half of my life: potential recognized, assistance offered, person taken advantage of, and bridge burned.

Life at home was about to change. After a few boyfriends, one of which lasted a couple of years, even though he grew and smoked marijuana in the house; my mom remarried when I was in the sixth grade. It seemed like a good move. The opposite of the pothead, my stepdad was a tenured college professor which meant that suddenly we had money! Just like that, we had name brand food like Kellogg's, Nestle and Kraft instead of the generic white boxes with black letters that simply stated what was in the container–"Corn Flakes," "Peanut Butter," or "Laundry Detergent." However, the vibe in the house didn't change and actually became worse when he started beating my mom. We had to pull him off of her a couple of times. He would move out but then quickly return. They stayed married for about 10 years before they divorced.

The same year they married; my mom smoked weed with me on my 12th birthday. True story. My reasoning was simple- I wanted to try it because I had been around it for so long. Her former pothead boyfriend grew weed in our home and smoking it in the house was his daily ritual. I had been bugging her to try it, so she wanted me to do it in a safe place–our home. So, I smoked a joint with my mom on my 12th birthday. Although I didn't feel much when I tried it, that first time gave me the green light to continue. Within a few years, I would become a daily weed smoker, right in the comfort of my own home- and I didn't see anything wrong with it.

Chapter 2

The Wonder Years

Every kid grapples with understanding who they are when they enter the teenage years, yet I also became very self-conscious and curious about my identity. I always wondered who my birth parents were. I knew I was adopted, because my parents told me as soon as I could comprehend. I guess it would have been hard to hide in my case, as my brother and sister are blondes and my mom was a redhead. Ironically, I actually look a little like my adoptive father, but it was clear, especially when the afro and the African American features emerged, that there was some "splainin" to do!

I was very self-conscious about my identity as a kid because I was the only black kid in my neighborhood. Although I had friends, I never felt fully "in." There was always the fear of the "hood" in Berkeley and Oakland that any kid from the hills would have, but as I got older I found that I liked hanging out with my Black friends at their home. There was a sense of warmth and acceptance that I would feel. In hindsight, I think that may have been because of the commonalities of race. Funny how I **never** thought that I was White, or even tried to be, despite the fact that I am half and half. I **always** identified as Black even before I could have expressed that. I just was. Even when the boxers would fight on Wide World of Sports back in the 70's, I ALWAYS rooted for the Black guy if a Black and White boxer were fighting. I guess we are attracted to what we see in the mirror over what our environment is; at least that's how it's always been for me.

I used to daydream that Walt "Clyde" Frazier was my father. He was the epitome of cool in the 1970's. Starting point guard for the New York Knicks, he was an NBA champion, a flashy dresser, and he always seemed to be smiling. I lay in my bed and imagined "Clyde" pulling up in a limousine, announcing to the entire neighborhood that he was my father, and whisking me off to a Manhattan penthouse where I would grow up rich and knowing where I came from. Sounded like a good deal, right? Unfortunately, it never happened, and I would awaken the next morning to the same reality. I still smile and reminisce about those childhood fantasies whenever I watch a Knicks game on NBA TV and "Clyde" is doing the commentary.

Religion was not a part of our household at all when I was growing up. No church, mosque, synagogue, nothing. God was not mentioned in our home unless used as part of a cuss word. I actually felt sorry for my friends who had to go to church or Hebrew school. I know now that they were receiving a foundation for their lives- a moral compass that would guide them through their journey. I had none of that. My mom loved Christmas, though. We always had a live tree and decorations around the house. She baked Christmas cookies and "stollen" which is a delicious cake-like fruit bread. Even in the lean years we had stockings and presents. We also had a little upright piano and she taught us how to read music a little. I could even play a hesitant Silent

Night. To this day I love everything about the celebration of Christmas and today I celebrate it on a deeper level as it recognizes the birth of my savior, Jesus Christ.

Jesus was never mentioned in our home though, except as part of Christmas songs. The impact of his birth and time here on earth were never explained to me when I was a child. To me, Christianity was epitomized by the preachers I saw on tv who looked like they were scamming people for money. The little I knew about Christianity and the bible was that it was a bunch of "thou shalts" and "thou shalt nots." No thanks! There were already enough rules and restrictions in life without adding more! So, I wrote off religion until later in life when I was desperate, and in enough pain, to do some seeking.

I will say, however, that I was never an atheist. Although I couldn't express it then, I always "knew" that there was an intelligent Designer or Creator of all of this. I knew nothing about the creation story, the fall of man, original sin, etc.; yet I knew this wasn't some "cosmic accident." I was also keenly aware of Someone watching over me, not in a spooky way, but in a protective, comforting way. It was very real for me, almost tangible. Psychologists might explain it as the yearning for safety of a child growing up in a fragile, unsafe home, and that may be, but I know what I felt. There was never a need to manufacture this "Protector" or stretch my imagination. It was simply knowledge like I know my right foot from my left, it just was. I believe God gifted me with this assurance at a very young age and it was foundational as I developed my faith later on in life.

High school, however, was a haze of smoking weed, cutting class, going to "keggers" and occasional schoolwork. Very early during my freshman year I discovered that if I had weed, I had friends! The problem was that pot made me extremely paranoid and self-conscious. All the "cool" kids did it though, so I was committed to mastering the marijuana-induced paranoia. I never did, which only magnified the already-awkward teen-aged years. Once, I went with a buddy to get our ears pierced, only the left ear, in an effort to be cool. They poked the hole in my ear and put in a giant earring that looked like a ball bearing. It had to be worn for a couple of weeks and then my ear could take any earring. I went home with this thing in my ear and instead of getting angry, my mom took one look at me and burst out laughing. That was way more effective. I took that pinball out of my ear and never wore an earring again.

I threw a party the summer before my senior year. To be more exact, a party was given, and my house was the location. I'd say at least 70% of the people there had NO idea whose house it was. That's just how it was in Berkeley. When word got out about a raging house party, EVERYBODY showed up. There was no such thing as invitation-only. This is how it all went down: My mom and stepdad went out of town for a week, so all during the week, I had a few people over here and there. There were never more than ten at the most, which was bad enough. The day before they were to return, I was cleaning the house to make it look like nothing had ever happened, when I received an unexpected phone call. It was one of the most popular kids in school asking if I wouldn't mind if they brought a keg over and have a small get-together. The second step of Alcoholics Anonymous reads: "Came to believe that a Power greater than myself could return me to sanity." I had a problem with that when I first encountered it, "Sanity? That's pretty dramatic!" However, when I found out that Sanity simply means "sound thinking" I had to admit, my thinking was never very sound. The party of '86 is yet another exhibit I could use to make that case. A sound thinker would never have agreed to allow a keg to be brought over on the eve of his parents return. So desperate was I to be popular, though, that I instantly agreed! Well, when they came over, there were **two** kegs **and** they were charging people at the door! They had turned my parents' home into a nightclub! There were cars and drunken teen-agers everywhere. Someone ransacked the house, stealing valuable family heirlooms that my mom could never replace. Two girls ran up to me and proudly announced that the police had been called but they had intercepted them outside and somehow persuaded them to leave. I heard numerous people ask, "Whose place is this anyway?" The party was in full swing when suddenly one of my buddies walked up to me looking like he had seen a ghost, "Those look like parental units, Jimmy." I looked up and my mom and stepdad were walking through the front door a day early with luggage in tow.

What an indescribable feeling of being busted red-handed. All I could do was get everyone out of the house as fast as I could. Of course, there were a few hard cases who didn't care that my parents were standing there in shock. They wanted their money back and were not leaving until they got it. The guys who had used me told me they didn't have the money and I actually had to go up to my room and use my tiny cash reserve to pay the dudes off so that they would leave and I could deal with my livid parents. By the time everyone left, the house was in shambles, things were missing, I was grounded for the entire month of August, and I was never allowed to stay home alone again. Trust destroyed.

Looking back, the month I was grounded was the best month of my teen-aged years. My mom let me go to the neighborhood playground, but I had to be home by 4pm, which was a virtual death-sentence in the summertime in California. However, I couldn't get into any trouble and I didn't smoke any weed at all for the entire month of August. I remember because I used to post my drug use record on my wall calendar like wins and losses. If I stayed clean it was a win and if I used it was a loss. Even as a lost teenaged kid I knew I was better off clean. Most months were, like, 8-22; 7-24, but in August of 1986 I went 31-0 and I felt fantastic.

All of that changed when I went back to Berkeley High School for my senior year. Drugs were everywhere. Weed, coke, acid, "shrooms," alcohol–you name it. I marvel today at the ease in which a bunch of 16-18-year-olds could acquire a keg or two of beer, take it to a local park or parentless home, and get wasted.

I started dating in my senior year too. I met a girl who I fell madly in love with, at my part-time job at Round Table Pizza. She was absolutely beautiful! Gorgeous, caramel-complexion and pretty from head to toe; I had no idea why she was with me! I still remember our first kiss, sitting across from each other after work in a booth. We leaned in and kissed, and boy oh boy! Fireworks galore. I was smitten. She, not so much. I was more of a hobby for her. I remember big-time "D-boys," (drug dealers), dropping her off and picking her up at work. I would inquire and she would just say they were friends from her 'hood. She lived on Apgar Street in West Oakland, a world away from the secluded Berkeley Hills where I grew up. She eventually dropped me, and I got another girlfriend, a White girl who just presented herself at my locker one day and invited me to a party. This relationship didn't last very long. The most memorable part of it was after I broke it off with her, she told me she was pregnant. I was a nervous wreck for about a week until her best friend stopped by Round Table one day and told me it wasn't true. She was just trying to get back at me for breaking up with her.

Through it all, the one constant was drug use. Being an addict, (suffering from the disease of addiction is very dichotomous), I knew I was a better person clean. I actually **enjoyed** being clean, but also liked getting high. I liked the feeling that as long as I had this bag of weed in my pocket, it didn't matter who rejected me or how awkward I felt. I knew how to get high, and that I would feel comforted in that moment.

Crack hit the bay area in the mid-80's, and the first couple of times I tried it I didn't even know what it was. In our senior year, a lot of the kids were snorting coke and I tried it a few times, but I never really liked it. Then I noticed a couple of my friends sprinkling "coke" on weed before rolling it up. I just thought this was a different way of doing it so I tried it, and I could take it or leave it. I had no idea this was actually the crack thing that was turning people into walking skeletons that I had read about in the Oakland Tribune. I would soon discover just how different this crack thing was once I got turned out on it. I was working my shift at Round Table and the store bartender came in. He was a little older than most of us and I kind of looked up to him. He would even slip me a beer in a soda cup here and there. He called me over and said, "You wanna try something?" I was always up for a high, so I followed him into the bathroom and into the stall. Once there, he pulled out a pipe made from aluminum foil and sprinkled some tobacco out of a cigarette into it. He then pulled out a small baggie with a rock-like substance in it. I asked, "Is that crack?" He kind of shrugged and broke some off and into the pipe. He showed me how to hit it and when I took a pull, my life changed forever. The high is indescribable. It was as if all the dopamine in my brain was released at the same time. Pure ecstasy and then I had the overwhelming urge to hit it again. This was to be the pattern for me off and on for the next 25 years. This 'high' would take me from the Berkeley Hills to a prison in Pennsylvania. This 'high' would alienate me from my family, bankrupt me time and time again, and lead me to sleep in homeless shelters, jail cells, and roach-infested 'trap-houses'. It was the most exhilarating feeling I had ever had, and I chased that first hit across the country and back for 25 years.

hapter 3

Rehab and Relapse

"I need help." The three words every addict mumbles as they sink deeper and deeper into the abyss of addiction. In my case it was over the phone to the intake specialist at the Drug Rehabilitation Program at Alta Bates Hospital in Berkeley. It was 3am on December 27, 1987. I was out of money and wishing I were dead. A commercial for the rehab came on tv so I dialed the number.

I had fallen into a nightmarish pattern since my high school graduation the previous June. I was introduced to crack in April and by June I was getting it any chance I could. In fact, the day of my graduation, I borrowed $20 from my best friend, (and his car), and went to Oakland to buy crack. I came back to the Berkeley Hills, smoked half of it, ran down to my graduation at the Greek Theater, an hour late, and walked the stage high on crack with a rock in my pocket.

Directly after my graduation I was fired from Round Table Pizza for stealing, so I got a job as a laborer with a construction company. I was paid every other Friday and by Sunday morning the money was all gone. I was living at home with no bills to speak of, so I was able to continue this miserable pattern ad nauseum. It is hard to describe the misery and emptiness I felt when I'd smoked my entire paycheck and had nothing to show for it yet crawling around on the floor searching for crack. I hadn't slept or eaten in a couple of days which just added to the hopelessness. I truly wished I would just die. The self-hatred I felt was all-encompassing. One time, years later, I literally beat myself up after a binge, punching myself in the face repeatedly so that the next day it was sore and lumpy. Perhaps the gambler who blows it all on a big pot can relate. This happened every single payday and led to the phone call that early morning a couple of days after Christmas 1987. They had space, and a few days later, I was admitted to my first rehab at the age of 18.

"Are there any newcomers here for the first time?" the secretary of the AA meeting was asking. I found out later that this is asked at every meeting but on that day, at my first meeting, and pretty self-centered, I thought he was speaking directly to me to put me on the spot. I tentatively raised my hand, "Uh, I'm James, I guess I'm an alcoholic, even though I mostly do drugs." "Hi James!!! Welcome!! Keep coming back, we need you!!!" boomed the overwhelming response from everyone there. I was shocked. I had never been this welcomed anywhere! I was embarrassed but I had to admit, I liked it. I had always felt like I didn't belong anywhere, so it felt really good to be welcomed and accepted. I turned 19 while in rehab and really got into the 12-step program. I got a sponsor and started talking with him frequently. I saw people staying clean and sober, but not just that, they were **enjoying** life without drinking or drugging. I saw that it could be done, and I wanted in!

I felt fantastic when I left rehab in early March of 1988. I had gained back the weight I'd lost as a crackhead, plus

I still had my car, my job, and girls seemed to like me. In my 19-year-old world, all was well. I went back to work as a laborer but this time my paychecks went into my bank account, not to the dealers. I got a call from a girl I met in rehab, when I slipped her my number while she was there visiting her brother. I couldn't believe it! I mean this girl was **fine**. True, she had a baby, no job, no car, and lived at home with her mom but so what? She was **fine**! We started hanging out and I was head over heels. I really thought we were going to get married and the whole bit. In other words, I thought we were monogamous, just me and her, forever! Unfortunately, she didn't get that memo and when I discovered I was just **one** of her boyfriends, my heart broke and I did what so many people who suffer from the insidious disease of addiction do. "I'll show **you**, I'll hurt **me**!" In other words, I went back out into the world of drinking and drugging. 24 more years of pain and misery, knowing where the solution was the entire time.

I relapsed in November of 1988, and by the summer of '89, my mom had had enough and kicked me out. My brother's foster family let me come live with them in Fremont, California, so I moved into a tiny converted closet. I started going to Laney College in Oakland and tried to get my life on track. Unfortunately, I couldn't stop using.

By December of 1989, I had dropped out of college in order to work fulltime and pay off the bad checks I had written the summer before to get crack. I was working two part-time jobs at the local mall in Fremont, one at a music store that sold tapes and CDs and the other at a video arcade, which was still a thing in the late '80s. I met a guy who hung out at the arcade named Stone and we started hanging out. Stone was from Chicago and since he was in the Gangster

Disciples and a martial arts black belt, I thought he was cool. He showed me how to dress "fly" and hit the club scene. We always "pre-gamed" before going to the club. This consisted of drinking a half-pint of Jose Cuervo tequila, each, which was enough to get us pleasantly buzzed but not sloppy. Stone also had a car and he didn't do drugs besides alcohol, so he was the perfect buddy for me, or so I thought.

We became popular at one particular club in Fremont. We were young and dressed nice plus we could dance so the girls liked us. Stone was very charismatic, and people just seemed to flock to him. I rode the wave and had a little of my own swagger. Neither one of us had much money though. Most of mine was going to paying off those bad checks, and Stone didn't have a job. He lived with his girlfriend until she kicked him out, then I think he lived in his car.

We started talking about ways to get money illicitly. Neither one of us were criminal masterminds and Stone kept saying how easy it is to rob people. I had never done anything like that and, looking back, I never needed to. The crimes I committed in my life were the result of either following someone else in an attempt to be accepted or desperation because I needed drugs. One early morning, we were leaving the club and walking home, because Stone had recently wrecked his car. We were pretty toasted, and we started talking about robbing someone. Suddenly we saw a Latino guy walking alone in front of us. Stone said, "That's him let's get him." As usual, I was desperate to be accepted and, wanting to prove myself, I ran ahead and took the lead.

I ran right up on the guy and tried to act menacing, "What's up man! Give me all your money!" Startled, the poor guy turned and saw two idiots up on him. He held up one hand in a surrendering posture and reached for his wallet with the other. "Ok, ok, I give you, I give you!" He was scared to death and gave us no resistance. He handed over his wallet and, as I turned to run, Stone reached around me and knocked the guy down with one punch; his hat flying off as his head snapped back. I actually stood there dumbfounded for a second because I couldn't believe he was able to get enough on the punch while reaching all the way around me. Also, it was totally unnecessary. We already had the wallet and were leaving. The victim's screams snapped me out of it, and we ran away laughing; me out of nervousness and Stone out of sheer joy. "Help me, help me!" Our victim's screams trailed us as we ran. We slowed to a walk after a while so as not to attract attention and counted the haul. Thirty dollars. I had just committed a strong-arm robbery for thirty bucks. We took the loot to Denny's and spent it on breakfast and a cab ride home.

I hate to admit it, but at the time, I didn't initially feel bad about what we had done. However, as the days went by, I felt more and more guilty about it. I think God gave me an extra dose of conscience. Today, I realize the effect of the trauma we inflicted on that poor guy. Years later, I was robbed at knifepoint in Washington DC and I'll tell you I was **scared**. I know now what a horrible act it was, but unfortunately it wasn't the last time I did it.

A couple of weeks later, we were back at our club, "giggin," which was Bay Area slang for having a good time. Things were going well. I was on the dance floor with a cutie who was giving me play. Suddenly her eyes got wide and before I could turn around to see what was going on, two cops grabbed me and pulled me right off the dancefloor! Dummies that we were, we should have noticed that the hat that flew off the guy's head when Stone hit him bore the name of the club on it. Our victim was the dishwasher! He spotted us and fingered us to his boss who called the cops. They separated Stone and I and began interviewing us. Stone, being a gangster denied everything. Me, being a kid from the Berkeley Hills, confessed everything and off to jail we went. Stone couldn't believe I had sold us out and I did feel like a dummy, but I also felt a sense of relief and conscience clearing. This and other events have given me the solid belief that a life of crime is not for me. I **always** feel guilty; I **always** get caught and I **always** fess up. I am also the world's worst liar; my facial expressions give me away every time.

"So, am I basically going to spend the night in jail?" I asked the officer who was transporting me to Santa Rita County jail. I could see him react like "Is this kid for real? He's got an armed robbery charge and he's talking about one night in jail?" But he just shrugged and said, "Yeah, probably." I asked him if it was really bad there. I was scared to death, and he said, "No, it's ok in there," and we spent the rest of the ride in silence. We arrived at Santa Rita which is about 20 miles east of Oakland and I was processed in. I was given some clothes and a rolled-up mattress and sheets. Off to my housing unit I went. I felt like I was in a nightmare, but I couldn't wake up. Walking into the housing unit all I could see were faces, in cell doors, watching me and they all looked like killers. I could not believe that this was happening. Kids from my neighborhood did not go to jail, they went to Yale! Yet here I was.

"Pop 44!" The CO (Corrections Officer) yelled to the control bubble. The door opened and I walked into my new home. I said "wassup" to the guy on the bottom bunk who sized me up with one glance and barely nodded his head. "I'm just gonna hop up here," I said unnecessarily. Where else but the top bunk was I going to go? I was just so nervous; I had no idea what to do or how to act. I quickly found out that for me it was best to be myself and not try to act like a tough guy. There are some **real** tough guys in jail, and I was not one of them. Thank God no one tried me in any way physically because at that point in my life I didn't really know much about defending myself. God's grace yet again.

Jail is a world of its own. Nothing about my previous life could have prepared me for it. To say it was scary is an understatement. I was **terrified**. Everybody looked like a killer to me and I had no idea how to act. My first day, I broke an unwritten law and sat with a white guy at chow. I didn't know any better, every other table was either full or the guys eating together were clearly friends, so I sat with a guy who was eating alone and happened to be white. I got some looks, but no one really commented.

As usual, I made friends on the basketball court. I could play a little and I had a couple of good games which instantly earned me some respect. One of the OG's started calling me Kenny Walker who was a light-skinned player for the New York Knicks at the time. The nickname made no sense to me as I didn't think our games were similar, just our skin tone, but I knew better than to argue the point.

I also started working out pretty heavy. I realized I was facing some serious time and that if convicted, I would go to an even scarier place by the name of San Quentin. If that would be my fate, I was pretty sure I would get beat up, molested, and killed if I didn't at least look like I could defend myself. Unfortunately, there were no weights in Santa Rita, but I quickly found out that convicts are extremely resourceful, and that you don't need weights to get a great workout in. The first trick I learned was that if I filled a 25-gallon trash can about a third of the way up with water, grabbed a handle while my partner grabbed the other, we could do some fantastic bicep work doing trash can curls. Then I was shown how to place a towel on the metal stairs above my head, jump up to catch the edge of the stairs and bingo: Pull-ups. I also filled up a plastic trash liner with water and did all kinds of arm and shoulder work. Tricep dips off the chairs were popular and I never realized how many ways you can do push-ups until I went to Santa Rita. Feet up on a chair and hands on the floor for declines, feet on the floor and hands on the chair for inclines. Opposing thumbs and index fingers together in the shape of a diamond and going down to the floor until my nose or chin was in the diamond and back up for diamond push-ups. Some guys would flip into a handstand against a wall and do push-ups that way. Squats for the legs, all manner of ab work and cardio; the possibilities were endless. You can even clench your fists as hard as you can while flexing your arms for a full minute- Try it! I never again needed a gym in order to get a good workout in.

As we started going to court, I realized how serious my charges were. Stone had prior convictions and was facing at least eight years while this was my first arrest. Also, the lawyer told us that the victim was swearing it was me who hit him, which was understandable since I was the one standing right in front of him yelling in his face. He probably couldn't believe that Stone could knock him down from that position either. With all these factors, it was decided that I take the whole "beef" since this was my first conviction. After about 90 days, the DA offered time-served and five years of probation. I jumped at that and was released, not really comprehending that from that moment on, I had a felony on my record.

hapter 4

Street Life

I discovered, very quickly upon my release from jail, that I was homeless. The family in Fremont had had enough, and I still was not welcome at my mom's house. Since my extended family in the area either didn't have room or didn't want the drama I would bring; I stood homeless in my own hometown. I was now 21 years old and this is what my life had added up to. While most of my childhood friends were off in college, I turned 19 in rehab, 21 in jail, and now the streets would become my home. Typical of my self-centered attitude, I blamed everyone but the culprit–me. I felt abandoned yet again, which was how I entered into the world. Perish the thought that I had orchestrated this mess that my life had become, because my choices forced the very people who loved me to have to turn away.

With no clear plan for my survival, I decided to get a ride to Berkeley with another inmate whose family had picked him up. The only direction that I had at the time was to at least get back to Berkeley, and that ride was my only option. The first thing I did was call my homies, Carl and D. They came and scooped me up and asked what I wanted to do. I responded, "Let's go to Russell Street!" Russell Street was the infamous drug strip in Berkeley, where crack was easy to come by. I did at least have some money, thanks to the family that I lived with in Fremont who had managed to get my last check from my job at the arcade. I managed to get fired from my other job at the music store for stealing cassettes a month before my arrest, so I couldn't count on any funds there. We pulled up and D hopped out to get the drugs. He was taking a little too long and Carl and I were starting to get worried. Just when we were about to get out and see what was going on, D walked up to the car looking angry. "What happened?" I asked. "Well this mother****er with the gun over there isn't trying to give me the money back!" We both looked at D stunned. That's when I realized he either had more heart than both of us put together or he was truly crazy. Apparently, he had given the guy money for drugs and he had pulled a gun on D and told him to get lost. Instead of doing what most of us would have done and stepping off with the quickness, D stood there and argued with the guy the whole time Carl and I were waiting. D was truly angry and kept saying the guy wasn't really "built like that," and that we should go get our money back. Carl and I talked him off that ledge and we went and got some beer.

Carl let me stay at the church where he was doing maintenance work, but that got played out quickly. From there, I went to live in the basement of D's mom's house. I slept in a sleeping bag on the dirt floor of the unattached basement. This actually went on for a couple of months until she had to have some work done and opened the basement to find all my stuff there. I came "home" from work that evening and saw all of my belongings in the back of D's Volkswagen Jetta. He drove me to my mom's house and knocked on the door himself and pleaded my case. He came back to the car shaking his head and all I could tell him was, "Thanks for trying, but I told you man." He drove me down to the local YMCA and I got a room.

I lived at the YMCA for a few months, but I don't think I ever gave them any rent after the initial move-in payment. Their record keeping wasn't the best. I kept waiting for them to say something, but they never did. I was working as a laborer and I was spending most of my money on drugs. They had old vending machines that always ate people's money, and when that happened you filled out a form for a refund. The vending company would pay everyone back every few months. The payment would be whatever you lost .50 cents in one small envelope, and $1.00 in another. One day, I was talking to the guy at the front desk and noticed that the box with all the pay envelopes was right under the counter. I was broke and needed lunch money so as soon as he went to the back for something I leaned over the counter, reached down and grabbed the box. I went upstairs to my room and looked. There were a **lot** of envelopes in there, probably $100 worth, which would cover my lunches for a while. The only problem was I was the worst criminal in the world. Instead of taking the change out and throwing the envelopes away, I left everything intact and put it in my dresser so I could just grab what I needed each day. One day, I came home from work and the front desk person gave me a funny look. I shrugged and went up to my room. I opened the door and saw that I had left the dresser drawer open with the money box in plain view. The cleaning lady who cleaned our rooms every day must have spotted it and alerted management because right away my room phone rang, and I was told to come downstairs. I was kicked out that night. Kicked out from the place I used to insult. Now I truly had nowhere to go and had no viable options. My parting gift was directions to a shelter that I could go to that night, so off I went.

There was a lot of irony in my homelessness. We used to "cap" on each other in high school and one of the insults would invariably be "Aw that's why your momma lives at the YMCA!" It was across the street from Berkeley High School and the people we saw coming out of there were obviously "losers" in our eyes; yet here I was. Later, when I got kicked out of the YMCA and was living in shelters, I would take showers at my old school, Willard Junior High. One day when I was in the public line to take a shower, I noticed one of the workers was a girl that I remembered from high school. I never really knew her, but her boyfriend and I never got along. When she saw me, she looked away and started singing the old David Bowie song, "Ch-ch-ch-ch-Changes…" That hurt.

The way it worked in Berkeley back then was the shelter rotated from site to site. It might be in a church basement for a month, and then a recreation gymnasium the next. We just showed up by a certain time, grabbed a mat, and if we were lucky, they had actual cots to sleep on. We took a shower and went to sleep, then we were awakened around 5:00-5:30am to be gone by 6. This was actually good for me because I was working construction and had to get up early. The only issue was where would I put my stuff for the day. I stashed my bag in the bushes one day and it was all gone when I returned. Most of the guys just carried their stuff around with them all day but since I was working, I didn't want to tote a big ole bag to work every day looking like I was homeless!

Eventually, the shelter workers got to know me, and they let me keep my stuff there during the day. It was obvious that I was one of the few people who was actually working, so they cut me some slack. You meet a lot of interesting people in a shelter. Some had mental health conditions, and some, like me, were there because of drug and alcohol addiction. Then there were those who were simply down on their luck. There was a white guy there we used to call "CEO," because he had a nice car, nice clothes, and a nice haircut. He didn't appear to drink or smoke, and never socialized with anyone. Every day, he got up, and went on his way. Someone finally asked him what his deal was, and he said, "I lost my corporate job and my wife divorced me. She got the house and I needed to save money, so I decided to come to the shelter." He was going out every day to look for work. One day he didn't come back to the shelter, so we figured he got a job and a place to live.

"James, come here for a minute please," the shelter worker, Debbie called out before I left one morning. "Yes, Ms. Debbie?" I responded. "There's a house in Oakland that houses homeless guys who are trying to do right. I've watched you for the last few months and I know you go to work every day; you don't cause trouble and I can recommend you to them if you like." A big smile broke across my face. "Yes, Ms. Debbie, thank you!" I went to work that day feeling like a miracle had occurred. She was right for the most part. My drug use had subsided considerably since by the time I got off work I was usually too tired to try to find my old buddies or go to Russell Street. My priority was to take the bus to wherever the soup kitchen was that night and make it to the shelter in time. The structure that was built into the shelter life was actually a good fit for me. I returned that evening and Ms. Debbie smiled and said, "Go see Father Fitzpatrick at this address tomorrow after work. We're going to miss you, James." "Thank you, Ms Debbie! I'll miss you too!"

The next day was a bright, sunny, perfect California day. After work, I went to the address in North Oakland, just over the border from South Berkeley. I met Father Fitzpatrick who quickly told me to call him "Fitz." He was a tall, portly Catholic Priest who ran the house which was sponsored by Notre Dame University. He never wore a priest collar and was the first "man-of-the-cloth" I had met who was really down to earth and approachable. After he introduced himself and told me I was recommended by Ms. Debbie he asked, "So, what's a young, able-bodied guy like you doing being homeless?" I didn't know this was going to be an interview! I thought I was just going to move in. I couldn't tell him the truth: "Well, I just recently got out of jail and I'm battling drug addiction," or so I thought. In hindsight, nothing I could have told him would have shocked him, but I thought he would take away the opportunity if I was honest. I just shrugged and looked down, "Just life I guess," I mumbled.

Fitz smiled the big smile I got to know so well and said, "'Just life' yes, yes, I can understand that. Well, James we'd be happy to have you if this is a situation you would want to be a part of." On the tour of the house, I saw I would be sharing a room with two other guys upstairs. There was a room downstairs that housed three other guys. Fitz had his own room and the two staff members shared a room. There was a big living room that looked like a palace of comfort compared to the shelter, and so much food in the kitchen that I couldn't believe it! The staff cooked for the men every night and laid out breakfast cereal and pastries on the dining room table every morning. After months in the shelter, it looked like paradise. I smiled back at him and said, "Yes, I really appreciate it!" Fitz told me that I could move in right away, but I asked him for one more night. I wanted to say goodbye to my friends at the shelter.

Fitz was a little surprised by that, but thought it spoke to my character. I had actually bonded with some of the guys at the shelter. I wasn't using much and I'm generally a good guy when not on drugs. I genuinely wanted to say goodbye and not just disappear, leaving them at the shelter. So, I spent one more night there. Ms. Debbie made me explain exactly why I was there that night. The next day I got up, went to work, and then moved into the "Fitz House" as we called it.

The cycle would continue at the "Fitz House"–potential recognized, assistance offered, person taken advantage of, and bridge burned. Everything started out fine, as I transitioned into the rhythm of the house pretty well. Everyone had to be up and out by 7am and we were not allowed back until 4pm. So, if you weren't working, you were out looking for employment. This was pre-internet, for the most part, so circling want ads in the newspaper, pounding the pavement and knocking on doors were still tried and true methods of job-searching. I was one of the guys in the house who already had a job, so I felt like I was a notch above the rest.

The staff woke us up and set out breakfast in the morning. It was really an exercise in humility and servanthood for them, because they were serving a bunch of homeless guys. Besides Fitz, there was Bruce who was very humble and down-to-earth. He was also a tad bit effeminate to be in a house full of testosterone, but we didn't hold that against him since he was so cool. Then there was Andy, who was a young bull. A true Irishman in temperament and look- medium height, broad-shouldered, and barrel-chested with a shock of reddish-blonde hair. We didn't really like Andy because his disdain for us was barely hidden, and painfully obvious to men who were used to people looking down on them. We had our antennas up and were sensitive to that kind of vibe. Andy and I had plenty of run-ins, but since Fitz was the final authority on everything, I could always go to him when Andy threw up roadblocks, which were usually just following the rules and guidelines of the house. Fitz was full of grace and mercy and that drove Andy crazy. Andy eventually succeeded in getting me kicked out, but it was after four or five failed attempts, which were all justifiable by the letter of the law.

For example, one rule of the house was that we were to save 75% of our paychecks until we had saved enough to move out. I wasn't really feeling that rule, so I campaigned for them to make an exception for me. My reasoning was that since I worked in construction, it was imperative that I get a car to work in a transient industry. Andy was dead set against it since the rule of the house was very clear and this would be an unfair exception just for me. I pled my case and Fitz and Bruce outvoted Andy, which didn't enamor me to him one bit. I saved up around $1,000 which was enough to get a "hooptie," and I went to a used car dealership in Oakland. I test drove a 1976 Mustang II which had a 302 V8 engine and a loud stereo system. I fell in love and bought it even though it overheated on the lot right after the test drive. That car would eventually take me from Oakland to Seattle, and then out to Washington DC overheating every 100 miles or so.

There was plenty of irony living at the Fitz House too. Once, they took us all to the home of a friend of the church, probably to show us homeless guys how the other side lived. The house was in the Berkeley Hills overlooking La Loma Park and as we rode in the old passenger van up the windy roads higher and higher into the hills, I wondered how the staff would respond if I told them I knew a shortcut which would get us there quicker. Once we got to the house, they took us out to the deck to behold the magnificent view of the Bay in the distance and the pristine park right below us. Again, I was tempted to tell them I played in that park hundreds of times growing up and that we could walk over to my mom's house in about 7 minutes. I looked at Andy and decided to keep my peace; why give him another reason to dislike me? Or maybe he would be happy that I had ruined my life so completely.

Once I got the car, it was on and popping. I ran into a girl named Cat who I had tried to get with back when I lived at the YMCA. Back then, I would occasionally walk down Shattuck Avenue to her apartment where we would chill and watch tv. Nothing more. She gave me no play then, but this time around, I had a car, some money, and the confidence of a 21-year-old. Cat was 28 with a 5-year-old son. She was a white girl who looked like Mary McDonnell from the movie, "Dances with Wolves," with an incredible body. Tall, slender, but very curvy. I could not believe she was feeling me, and she was, without a doubt. I started hanging out at her place all the time. I even told the staff at the Fitz House about her. We were getting serious, telling each other we were in love. I explored moving in with her, but she stopped that real quick, as she told me that she was in the apartment under Section 8 housing and paying maybe $50 a month. She and her son would be kicked out If they found out an able-bodied man with a job was living there, and she would be taken off the Section 8 list and forced to pay market rent. Not happening. I was cool with that and kept hanging with her.

One day, as we were laying in the bedroom, something caught my eye in her closet. I asked her, "What's that?" Cat reached over and pulled a shotgun out of her closet. "A girl has to protect herself you know?" Guns always scared me, but I tried to play it cool, "Oh yeah, no doubt. Let me see that." She handed it to me, and not thinking, I pointed it right at her. "Stop, it's freaking loaded!" she screamed as she pushed it away. "Don't ever point a gun at someone unless you're going to use it!" I was in shock as the reality of what could have happened set in. I learned the Don't Point A Gun lesson that day and also another one: You never know who has a deadly weapon or where it might be.

As time went on, even though there was a zero-tolerance policy at the Fitz House, I started sneaking around drinking and using drugs. It was curtailed somewhat because of the house restrictions but I always found a way around it. One day I was smoking crack with my buddies and realized I had to get home. I made it back in time and left the rest of the drugs in my car. I went inside but that crack kept calling me. Once in the house you weren't supposed to go back out unless you had a pass or permission. I came up with about five different reasons why I had to go back out to my car. Then, after everyone went to bed, I got up three more times in the middle of the night and snuck outside to take a blast. Unfortunately, the last time I went out, I locked myself out of the house. It was 3am and I was outside, so I knocked on the only window I could get to which was Fitz's bedroom! He let me in the back door, but I noticed he was standing at the door completely naked. I don't know if he was angry or what the deal was, and I asked no questions. I just squeezed by and went upstairs. I believe that was the beginning of the end for me at the Fitz House.

Not long after my lockout incident, I woke up very sick. Cat and her son had been sick, and I thought that I probably caught it from them. I had a fever, the chills, a sore throat, the works. I knew I couldn't go to work but I had never tried to stay home before so I wasn't sure if I could. To make matters worse, Fitz was out of town and Andy was in charge. I stumbled downstairs and asked him, "Hey, I'm really sick, man. Can I stay home today?" He replied, "Absolutely not! You know the house rules. Everyone leaves!" "But Andy, I'm **really** sick, like no joke, I feel horrible man, and there's no way I can go to work like this!" Have you ever talked to someone and knew that whatever you were saying was falling on deaf ears? Like my words were just bouncing off the wall and back in my face. Andy probably knew I was using. He also knew they had made an exception to the rules allowing me to buy a car before I moved out. The staff had even bought me things for my car for Christmas like a tire gauge, oil, and antifreeze. Andy knew that I had taken all of this kindness and did what I wanted to do anyway. He was probably sick of my crap, and I believe that he was also a little jealous having no girlfriend or car of his own. In his eyes, this homeless guy was living a pretty good life with a fine girlfriend right under his nose. I had seen him around girls, and he was pretty awkward so there may have been some envy intertwined with just being fed up with my shenanigans. With all this in play, Andy said, "I don't care if you go to work but you have to leave the house **now**!"

I think it was his authoritative tone that set me off. "F*** you!" I screamed as I swiped all of the cereal boxes off the table. I forgot that the staff opened them all as a courtesy to us, so seven boxes of cereal flew off the table with the contents going everywhere. I kept moving as I swiped the boxes off the table and walked out of the dining room towards the front door; but I caught a glimpse of what I had done. There was cereal everywhere. I mean this was a real mess and it was bad. Andy was dumbfounded. He just stood there with his mouth gaping. I looked back at him and I saw shock, but beneath it I saw something else- satisfaction.

I left and went to Cat's apartment. Cat and her son were just getting over what I had so she wasn't too happy about me being there with my contagious germs. I was quarantined to the living room couch while they hid in their rooms, and after a while, Cat came out and asked what happened. After I ran the situation down to her and that I might be getting kicked out of the Fitz House, she reiterated that I couldn't stay there and maybe I should go to the hospital, because: a) I looked terrible and, b) a doctor's note might get me back in the Fitz House. Off to the hospital I went.

The doctor confirmed that I was really sick, with a temperature of 103 and all the symptoms of the flu bug that was going around. She wrote the diagnosis down and I went back to the Fitz House armed with the note. Bruce answered the door and he couldn't even look at me. He told me to wait and he went and got Andy. Andy came up to the door and just shook his head when I tried to hand him the note. He wouldn't even look at it. He said, "You're out of here until Fitz gets back. Come back in two days." Then he slammed the door in my face.

Back at Cat's place I wasn't doing great either. She was not happy about a deathly sick guy crashing on her sofa for two days, but she let me. I was feeling a little better when I went back to the Fitz House two days later, and I felt that Fitz would give me another chance. The staff and I sat around the dining room table and it was pretty clear the decision was already made, that this was just a formality. When I tried to show Fitz the doctor's note, he barely glanced at it. He began, "Jim, stop hiding behind your sickness. A lot of people get sick without exhibiting the violence you displayed the other morning. Do you know how long it took Andy to clean up all that cereal? Andy also says that George, (another resident), saw a car like yours circling the block last night. Were you trying to intimidate us?" "Fitz I've been laying down sick on Cat's sofa for the last two days. That wasn't my car," I replied. Andy chimed in, "Yes it was and why don't you just move in with your girlfriend?" "I can't," I replied, "she'll lose her apartment. Please guys. I know I made a terrible mistake. I had a temperature of 103 and I just lost it. I'm really sorry. It will never happen again. Please let me come back."

Fitz was sitting across the table shaking his head, "No, Jim, we can't do it. We suspect you've been breaking the house sobriety rules for a while and this is the last straw. I'm sorry but you need to gather your things and leave immediately." I looked at them; Fitz and Bruce actually looked sorry. Andy was smirking like he was holding in a belly laugh. "He finally got me," I thought. "This is messed up, man," I said. "You're kicking out a guy who just got out of the hospital. Ok, I'm gone." I didn't have the energy to argue, and at the end of the day, I had been taking advantage of their kindness for a while. It had just caught up with me. The other residents didn't seem too sad that I was leaving either, so I guess I had been pretty full of myself with my job, car, and pretty girl.

I went back to Cat's and broke the news, "Well they kicked me out," I said. "You can't stay here," she replied immediately. "Just tonight and then you have to go." "Wow," I thought, "How quickly things can change." I spent the night on the couch and then it was back to the shelter life. I'll never forget the look of disappointment on Ms. Debbie's face when I straggled into the church basement the next night.

hapter 5

An Unlikely Change

Here I was **back** in the shelter, but I still had my job and my car. Cat dumped me. I went past her place about a week later and some other guy was in there. She didn't even answer my knock at first, but her son saw me out of the window and started yelling "Hi Jimmy, Hi Jimmy!" She opened the door and let me in. It was a pretty awkward two minutes as this Rico Suave look-a-like and I stared each other down while Cat showed me to the door. I didn't even have the heart to protest how quickly she was replacing me; I just walked away.

Having a car definitely helped me get around a lot easier but it also opened up time for me to use drugs since I didn't have to walk everywhere or time the busses. My drug usage became worse, yet I went to work just about every day, because they kicked us out of the shelter at 6am and I didn't have anywhere else to go. Life went on like this for a few months–I woke up, went to work, went to whatever church had the free dinner that night, and then to the shelter. If there was time, and I had money, I would buy crack and a 40 oz bottle of Olde English 800 so I could come down from the crack high and not be "geeking," which meant craving for more drugs. I didn't want to show signs of weakness in the shelter, so I tried not to use too much. However, it started getting bad, especially on the weekends. I was really running out of hope. I knew AA was waiting for me and that I could get sober going to the meetings, but I just loved getting high too much.

I met a guy named Dave in the shelter. He was a white guy, maybe 40 years old, with curly brown hair and a quick salesman's smile. He made you feel good with his positive attitude and good vibes. Dave latched on to me, probably because I had a car, and we started hanging. He didn't use drugs at all and didn't drink much either, but I found out what his deal was–Dave was a degenerate gambler. He had lost his beautiful family and been kicked out of every place he lived because of his gambling addiction. Getting to know Dave really showed me how destructive a gambling habit can be. It can be just as bad as drugs. He and I would ride around and talk, and he filled my head with ideas about the big pots he had won at the poker table and how he just had a string of bad luck. Now he knew what mistakes he had made and if he ever got a stake again, he would turn it into riches. It sounded good to me!

One day, Dave told me he was going to confide something in me that I couldn't tell anyone. He knew of a poker game just outside of Seattle, Washington where he had won big before. He said he won so much money that it ruined his life. I asked him what he meant by that, and he explained. His wife and daughter lived up there, and after he won, he didn't come home for weeks living the high life. When he did come home, his wife kicked him out. He said if he could just get back up there, he would win big again, and of course, he would reward me if I helped him get back there. Well, he didn't have to ask me twice. Life was going nowhere for me in March of 1991. I was 22 years old, homeless, with a drug habit and a felony conviction. I figured no one would even miss me or, probably more accurately, I hoped that they would miss me and regret ever treating me this way. So, I quit my job and we threw our meager belongings in my old Mustang II and headed up the highway.

We drove north to Tukwila, WA, just outside of Seattle, in a day and a half. The first stop Dave made was his ex-wife's house. We didn't stay there long, and I got the impression he wasn't very welcome. We got a hotel suite and sat down to figure out our next move. The poker game Dave was so hyped about was in a couple of days, so we decided to relax and enjoy a couple of days living in a nice hotel suite, a bit different from being surrounded by 100 other dudes in a shelter. The only money that we had was from my last paycheck from my construction job, yet we weren't worried at all. Dave convinced me that we were going to be rich in a couple of days.

That Friday night we walked down to the restaurant, which also housed the gambling spot. Dave was happy as could be and I was riding the wave of his emotion. I still had the need for acceptance and whenever someone accepted me, I would follow them loyally, even if he was a degenerate gambler I met in a homeless shelter. We arrived at the spot and they obviously knew Dave. They welcomed him and took him right to the poker game. I grabbed something to eat and stayed out of the way. After about an hour, I walked over and checked in on Dave. He didn't look so happy, but when he saw me, he pasted that quick smile on his face. "Taking a little longer than I thought Big Guy." He gave me $5 and told me to get a drink while he worked his magic. The other players were trying to look neutral, but their smirks were unmistakable. I had a sinking, helpless feeling as I walked away and waited. After another hour, Dave came up to me looking really sheepish. "Wow Big Guy, I had 'em at first but then I just couldn't get the cards I needed. Lost it all Big Guy, lost it all." I just stared at him.

As a child, I had lost my voice. The "voice" is what people use when they need to state and defend opinions and beliefs. It is also used to defend or stand up for oneself. That voice was slapped, bullied, patronized, and ridiculed out of me very early in life. I remember when I started finding my voice again: I was in my forties and working in the professional world. I realized, quickly, that if I didn't find my voice, I would not make it through staff meetings, networking events, and other settings where my opinion and the defense of it were expected. I sheepishly started testing my voice, and after a few years, became pretty comfortable with it!

However, in 1991 at the tender age of 22, fresh out of the shelter and off crack for about a week, I had no voice. I just looked at Dave, hoping he was joking but knowing he wasn't. "I'm sorry Big Guy, I know I can get 'em though! Just have to get another bankroll!" I just shook my head and walked back to the hotel with Dave yapping in my ear the whole way. Once back in our fancy suite, reality set in. We were paid up through the week but had no more money. We were all in on that poker game and we had lost. "We need jobs, Dave," I stated. He looked like I had slapped him or said a cuss word. His face went through different emotions: shock, amusement, incredulity, and finally, resignation. "Yup," he nodded, "I guess you're right."

Dave knew of a day-labor place, so we went and started working hard. We were laborers helping to gut a huge warehouse that was being converted into something else. All day we were knocking down walls and ceilings, putting the scraps in wheelbarrows and 20-gallon trash cans, and carrying everything out and dumping it in a dumpster. One of the funniest sights I've ever seen was Dave, who owned nothing but slacks and dress shirts, working hard manual labor all dressed up, sweating while still trying to smile and laugh all day. By the end of the first day, his smile was forced, and his pretty clothes were dripping with sweat. I had to force him out of bed the next morning so we could do it all again. We did this for a couple of weeks and applied for other jobs when we were off. After about two weeks, Denny's called, and I interviewed for a job as a dishwasher/busboy. I landed the gig and Dave promptly quit the day labor job since I was his ride and there was no way he was taking the bus.

I realized, far too late, that Dave was a loser. He took his day labor earnings back to the gambling spot and lost it. He was going to ride it out as long as I let him, losing his money and depending on me to pay the rent. Luckily, I had my own ace up my sleeve, so to speak. I had cousins who lived in Bellevue, WA and I gave them a call. We were pretty close with them, since us kids even flew up there and lived with them for about a month when I was in the fourth grade. I called my aunt and uncle, (actually my "aunt" is my mom's cousin), and I told them I was in the area working but I needed somewhere to live. They met me at a restaurant so they could check to see if I was drugged out. I had been "clean" since leaving California, now only having the occasional beer. Since I looked ok, they agreed to let me stay with them temporarily. I moved to their basement sofa and continued working at Denny's, never to hear from Dave again.

It's funny how an addict can find drugs. You can drop a real addict into any city, anywhere in the world, and within an hour or so they will find what they want. Looking back, I am amazed and horrified at some of the places that I went in hopes of getting dope. I would drive around until I found the "hood" then find a crackhead to direct me to the dealers. I've been robbed a few times and had people just straight up run off with my money, but it never stopped me from my quest. It never helped that I am obviously a guy from the Berkeley Hills, and always stuck out like a sore thumb. People actually thinking that I was a police officer probably saved me more times than I realize or care to admit.

The point is, I was doing pretty well at my cousins', working, saving money, but that itch came back. Everyone who has ever struggled with addiction, be it drugs, alcohol, sex, gambling, shopping, knows the itch. This is what some call, "The insanity of the first drink." I got the idea in my head to get high and that was it. I knew the outcome was not going to be good. I knew I would end up broke, and I knew it was a stupid thing to do but once that idea is planted, unless there are tools in place, an active relationship with God, and, in my opinion, a robust commitment to a 12-step program; the addict does not stand a chance. That is probably the most misunderstood aspect about the dynamic of addiction. People think we are choosing the substance over them, but choice is not in the picture. Once thoroughly addicted, no amount of willpower will manage a healthy sobriety for a sustained period of time. Oh, an addict might get clean by "white knuckling" it, but that's known as a "dry-drunk" and they are the most miserable of creatures. Clean with no recovery. It's usually only a matter of time before they use again, shop again, gamble again etc. When I hear people say they "just stopped" but there are no meetings, no development of a relationship with their higher power, no support system, and they can't tell you their "clean date," which is their first day clean after their last drink, drug, gamble, inappropriate sex, etc. I usually steer clear of those people. They may be "clean," but they are probably not healthy mentally, emotionally or spiritually.

One night I got my paycheck, that itch got me, and with nothing in place to combat it, I got in my car and drove the 10 miles or so to Seattle. I found the hood immediately, connected with another addict, and was back in Bellevue with crack within an hour. After I finished that, I went back and found the same guy. I repeated this twice more before I was out of money. Luckily, I had been giving my aunt my money to keep and I didn't have the nerve to ask her for it at 4am, so I "geeked" for an hour or so and went to sleep.

A few days later, my aunt sat down and talked to me about my future there, which was the hard reality that I didn't have one. I'm sure she noticed that I didn't give her that last check, and she was no dummy. She told me about a place called Doe Bay, which was a resort on Orcas Island, where many young people went to work and figure things out. Orcas Island is part of the San Juan Islands off the coast of Washington. There are quite a few resorts on Orcas Island, and Doe Bay, by far, was the most rustic. Young people would go there and work for a small stipend plus room and board. The room and board usually meant that you needed to bring a tent, which I did. If you had seniority you slept in your own cabin and if you were good with your hands, you could build your own wigwam, which is a natural shelter made from saplings, bark and leaves. I had my little tent, which was good enough for me, even though I envied the guys who built their own wigwams. Somehow, I was too embarrassed to ask for help building my own.

For work, we all cleaned the guest cabins in the mornings and had another job in the afternoons. I learned how to kayak and became a guide, even though I was a beginner. I also worked in the Vegetarian Café and became a pretty good short-order cook specializing in stir-fry veggies and tofu. At night we drank liquor and smoked lots of weed while sitting around campfires playing guitars and bongos and singing drunken songs. The nights were very clear, and I even learned some of the star constellations.

Doe Bay was good for me, I was no longer smoking crack, but eventually there were just too many of us young people running around for them to keep paying. I met a guy there named Sam and we became friends. Sam was cool. I liked him because he knew about sports and other regular things that most of the hippie type guys there didn't know anything about. When they stopped paying us, Sam suggested I come out to Maryland where he lived and help him and his brother with their landscaping company. He already had a plane ticket but said he would meet me there in eight days. Sounds good to me! I didn't want to go back to California because I knew what would happen as soon as I got to Berkeley, so this seemed like a good option. The plan was to work with them for the summer, save money, then go down to Florida to get a job on a cruise ship and see the world. I guess that my time there served its purpose, because for the first time, I had an actual plan.

I also told my plan to a girl I had been trying to "mack" ever since she stepped foot on Doe Bay. She was of Indian descent, very beautiful, and very sweet, but she was not going for my advances at all! I told her that I was off on an adventure driving across the country and that she should come. She was all for it, but there was a catch, her best friend, and her best friend's brother, who were at Doe Bay with her had to come. They would go as far as Wisconsin and then I would continue to Maryland. I said, "okay," only because I thought it would give me a chance with her. So, we packed our belongings onto the roof and trunk of my '76 Mustang II, stuffed four people in the car and took off.

Predictably the car overheated constantly. After two days, we had only made it to Coeur d'Alene, Idaho. Setting up in the campsite where we were sleeping that night, I knew this wasn't going to work. I told her that her friends had to go, because it was just too much weight. Well she made it known that she was not driving across the country with just me, and she would leave with them. The next morning, we drove back to Spokane, WA since it had the nearest bus station and they got out. It was an awkward and terrible drive, because they were all really upset with me. They had to call their parents to get money wired to them so they could buy bus tickets. I unloaded my passengers and all of their belongings with a feeling of relief as I hit the road again. The old Mustang II seemed relieved too! Along with unloading all that weight, I went and bought a new radiator cap and it went from overheating every 50 miles to every 400-500 miles. I was in Spokane, WA heading for Rockville, MD 2,500 miles away. I had a 15-year-old car, a lingering drug habit, and $300 in my pocket. Let's go!

hapter 6

A Brand-New Start

I quickly deduced that with $300, I was not going to be able to sleep in any hotels along the way. Also, buying gas was going to hinder my bankroll. So once again, I took what I wanted. From Spokane, Washington to Rockville, Maryland, I spent around $25 on gas. This was 1991 when the average price of gas was $1.14 a gallon, but still, there's no way $25 would get me 2,500 miles across the country. I realized that at many of the gas stations in the small towns across the country you could pump first and pay afterwards. I always chose stations that were just off the highway, so that I could pump my gas, jump right back in my car, and get right back on the highway. There were no cameras in those days, and I guess most of the attendants didn't care enough to report it. The only times I paid was when the attendant would actually come outside and watch me. In that case I would pump $5.00 or so and then go to a station a few exits down.

This still left little money to stay at a hotel or motel, so I parked at rest stops and pitched my little tent in the surrounding woods. I found out I could shower at truck stops so that helped me to stay somewhat clean. My food supply was pretty well stocked, thanks to raiding the stockroom before I left Doe Bay. This meant I only had to buy sodas and coffee along the way. Drinking and drugging never entered my mind on the trip. I knew there was no wiggle room financially and I did not want to become stranded somewhere in Iowa, broke from a crack binge.

It's funny how I could have laser-like focus provided I had just a little direction. I had a goal: Maryland. I also had complete trust in Sam. Why would he make this kind of promise and not follow through? I had his home number and the day he was to be home, so I was good to go. It's pretty incredible, as I look back, how I had one hundred percent confidence in everyone but myself. For some reason, I just felt like everyone else pretty much had life figured out while I was flopping around barely treading water. If you sounded confident and made sense, I would follow you until the wheels fell off which they usually did.

I also marvel at the stamina I had back then. These days, in my fifties, a three to four-hour drive pretty much wipes me out. Back then, I could literally drive 10, 12, 14 hours at a clip. Just give me some good tunes on the radio, a tank of gas and I'm good. I remember the beautiful scenery of Montana and Wyoming. Montana was definitely Big Sky Country filled with a dome of millions of stars at night, but Wyoming's peaceful skies with their array of beautiful colors impressed me even more. The miles upon miles of wide-open spaces actually shocked me. My first thought was "How are there any homeless people in this country? The government could just slap little communities together in these empty spaces and move all the homeless in!" I was surprised at how friendly the people were in Iowa of all places. I mean, they were so nice. I figured they'd be like, "Ok here's a young black kid with California tags. What is he doing here?" But I was wrong. They were genuinely friendly and made a point to greet a stranger and a friend alike. Since these were the days before GPS, they were also very patient about giving directions. Kansas was flat. I mean just long stretches of flat highway. Easy driving. I had three tapes I kept playing over and over, The Doobie Brothers, Marvin Gaye, and The Temptations. All great driving music.

When I grew tired of my tapes, I found the local radio stations. There were some parts of the country where all I could get was Country or Classical music. As a result, I grew to appreciate both. For some reason, though, Classic Rock became my go-to driving music. Something about the smooth melodies and catchy tunes. I also loved Classic R & B and Hip-Hop that I could sing/rap along to which passed the time easily and smoothly. As I get older, I still love all these genres plus Gospel, however I am also developing an affinity for Jazz which I never expected.

As I got closer to Maryland, I realized I was ahead of schedule. I called Sam who was still at Doe Bay and he confirmed he wasn't due for four more days. So, I found a KOA campsite near Harper's Ferry, WV which is about 50 miles from Rockville, MD. KOA is a chain of campgrounds that are all across the USA. They're clean, well-kept, very inexpensive, and always have a swimming pool. Back then it was around $14 a night. Not a problem. I still had over $200 from being so "crafty" getting gas during my trip across the country. I pulled in, paid my fare and pitched my tent.

I slept most of the first day away, but then I got antsy and bored. Being 22, I was always looking for some action, so I started exploring. My first stop was the swimming pool, since I figured there would be women there. They were definitely there, but mostly middle-aged with husbands and kids. I quickly realized that the KOA campground was not the hot singles scene. It was full of families doing their summer vacation thing. I realized this was going to be a long four days.

There was one woman I met there. She was single, a little older than me, probably in her late 20s with a four-year-old son. She was very attractive with dark hair and a beautiful smile. She was also a Christian; like a real Jesus-loving Christian. This was a new species to me. Berkeley was one of the most godless places on earth. Full of intellectuals, hippies, and students, organized religion was largely frowned upon and looked at as a sign of weakness. Having never been introduced to any religion growing up, I figured what I heard people say was true that it was all just a way to control people and get their money. Growing up in the Hills, most of my neighborhood friends were either Jewish or Catholic, and they behaved pretty much as I did. They just had more constraints and rules to follow. I was guilty of what most people who laugh at Christians are: contempt prior to real investigation.

This young woman noticed that I was always alone, so she struck up a conversation with me. Of course, I immediately concluded that she wanted me and found me irresistible. She invited me over to her campsite for dinner with her and her son, so of course I went! We had dinner and then she said, "We're going over to the rec hall. A few of us have bible study every night around this time." So that's her game! I was disappointed but not yet defeated. If that's what it was going to take to get next to her, hey, let's do this! We walked over to the rec hall and were greeted there by six or seven others. Mostly men. "Uh-oh, they want her too," I thought.

She introduced me around and everyone greeted me with warm genuineness. "Fake," I thought. "They're supposed to act like this." We gathered in an informal circle and sang some songs out of a hymnal. I felt like an utter fraud. The songs were totally unfamiliar, and I knew I was a hypocrite singing about a God I knew nothing about and who probably didn't have time or inclination to think about me. After we finished, we took turns reading the bible and the leader stopped us periodically to explain what we were reading. I kept glancing at my "date," who at this point, was totally engrossed in the reading, smiling and nodding her head as it was explained. "She's really gone," I thought. "Brainwashed." After it was over, we milled around a bit and everyone hugged it out and spilt up. My "date" asked me, "What did you think?" "It was nice!" I lied. I could tell she saw right through me, but instead of being angry, the look she gave me was unmistakable: Pity. Honest to goodness pity that I wasn't getting it, and that I wasn't experiencing the love of God that she was walking in. Worse yet, I wasn't the slightest bit interested in it either. "Will you join us tomorrow?" she asked. "I'll try," I lied as I turned and walked back to my lonely tent. I never went back, but it's funny how that small encounter left such an impression on me. I couldn't deny that these people really believed in this thing and there was an inner peace and joy that exuded from them. I still thought it was kind of fake, but I couldn't deny there was something there. I felt empty. I wished I could have some of their joy and peace, yet I thought I was too far away from anything like that. It was pointless to even try.

After four days, I called Sam and he was finally home. He gave me directions and I made my way to Rockville. Montgomery County, MD wasn't totally foreign to me. I was in the sixth grade when my mom got married to a college professor who split his time between teaching anthropology at George Washington University in Washington DC and Berkeley. When I was about to enter the eighth grade, they decided to try a full year on the east coast. The four of us, me, my sister, Mom, and her husband, moved to Bethesda, MD where I attended Thomas Pyle Jr. High School for my eighth-grade year. It was actually a good year for me, and I made a lot of friends in Bethesda; however, we were all homesick for California, so we went back home after that one year.

When Sam mentioned Rockville, back in Doe Bay, I knew exactly what and where he was talking about. Bethesda and Rockville are only about eight miles apart. I guess that alleviated any hesitancy I might have had about giving it a try. When I touched down at his parents' house in early July 1991, I was very optimistic. Sam put me up in one of the bedrooms and assured me that all was cool with his parents who were summering in Maine and wouldn't be back for a month or so.

We started working with his brother, Paul the very next Monday. Landscaping is a whole different animal in Maryland; it's big business. Actually, what we were doing could have been considered lawn care. Paul had built his business up very well. He had a brand-new 300-ZX, which was the "hot car" at the time, and he also had a brand-new pickup truck that pulled the trailer which held three top-of-the line lawn mowers. These weren't the push mowers that I struggled with to mow our backyard as a child. These were gas powered, commercial lawn care machines that you walked behind or stood on the pedal and rode. I was able to get the hang of the mowers and trimmers pretty quickly, so Sam and I took over the route. Paul was happy with that since it gave him the opportunity to now sit at home with his girlfriend and collect money while we worked in the hot, humid Maryland summer. The third worker was Paul's German Shepherd, Fritz, who rode along with us. Fritz was a great dog, and the reason I love German Shepherds to this day.

As the days rolled on, I started to notice that Sam and Paul didn't really get along. They were always bickering, yet it seemed to me that Sam didn't respect Paul's position as the owner of the business. He was, after all, the boss. After about a month or so, Sam quit, and Paul gave me a two dollar an hour increase to work the route alone. I was happy with that arrangement and Fritz and I went out every day except when we got rained out. Sam wasn't mad at all. He got another job and there was no awkwardness between us at the house. We even hung out and went clubbing in DC a few times. We would drink and maybe smoke some weed if one of his friends had it but no hard stuff. I was finally feeling like I had escaped crack for good.

One night, Sam took me down to DC to his friend, Gary's place. He was quite the character. Gary was older than us, around 40 at the time, but had more energy than anyone I'd ever met. A small black man around 5'7" and 145 pounds, Gary could out-drink, out-dance, out-talk, out-fight, and out-joke everybody. I am not exaggerating. A bigger-than-life personality who everyone wanted to be around, he had an apartment in the upscale Foggy Bottom area of DC just on the outskirts of Georgetown and walking distance to all the nightclubs. This presented the perfect spot to "pregame" before hitting the clubs. Gary and I hit it off immediately and I was happy to meet someone who I could relate to and who liked to party. This began a 20-year friendship that ended when I got sober and severed ties with him.

My living arrangements in Rockville were beginning to get a bit shaky. Sam's parents came home, and it was crystal clear that they had no idea who I was or why I was there. Sam tried to tell me that he told them, and they just forgot. Even I didn't believe that one. His mom was nice and understanding, but his dad was not having this arrangement at all. I also got a racist vibe from him which surprised me since I never caught an inkling of that from Sam or his brother. I thought back to the first time I was called a nigger by a white person, which was also in Maryland. I was in the eighth grade at Thomas Pyle Jr High and this white kid named Brett and I were teasing each other in drama class. I said something that cut him, and everything changed. He looked at me with hatred in his eyes and literally screamed, "You nigger!" right in my face. The teacher wasn't around so all the other kids, all of them white, looked to see my reaction. This was totally new territory for me. Growing up in Berkeley, all the ethnicities mixed pretty fluidly, and we all had friends of different nationalities. There were even some white boys who were cool enough to get a "pass," meaning they knew how and when to use the word, "nigga" and not get beat down.

This was something entirely different. I looked right into the face of racism that day, and not having a voice yet, I froze. I know many people will say, "I woulda beat his tail," and that might be true; but I was not equipped, in a room full of white people, in a strange town, with no sense of self, to lash out. I just stared at him in shock. That's when he started laughing. Not a friendly, "I'm just kidding" laugh. More of an evil, sinister laugh of one who knows he has the power and privilege to get away with what he just did. One of the girls said, "Brett, just shut up," and everyone kind of returned to other activities and conversations. I remember a group of us talking about it later and one of the girls saying, "Yeah, my dad is really racist too." That's when I realized I wasn't in Berkeley anymore. It was 1983 and racism was still alive and kicking in Maryland, much as it is today. It was also being modeled, taught, and passed down to the kids of my generation. I could tell that most of the white kids at Thomas Pyle weren't racist, at least not on the surface, but when they felt threatened, it came out much like Brett. If you had asked me before that day if he was racist, I would have laughed, "Of course not! Who has time to be a racist?" However, when push came to shove, it came out.

From that day on, my antenna was always up, and I stopped believing the surface façade. I no longer gave them the benefit of the doubt. Now white people were all suspect until they proved otherwise. What a paradox to have to live with while being raised in a white family! Today, I live in the space most people of color in America find themselves. We give you the benefit of the doubt because it's just too exhausting to walk around on defense all the time. However, our antennas are up. These antennas have been developed through trauma and abuse, not by choice. Some trauma has been minimal, like mine. Some trauma has been violent, nasty, mean, and unjust, to the point of loss of life for no other reason than the melanin in one's skin. Once I get a racist vibe from someone, they may not realize it, but they are under investigation until they prove that whatever alarm they set off for me was an honest mistake.

Sam's dad triggered my alarm. There was something deeper than his valid anger about having this strange guy in his house. Sam probably thought he would be ok with it after he got over the initial surprise, but he wasn't. Not at all. It was clear that I needed to get the heck out of there, and fast.

I found a room to rent in Gaithersburg which was the next town over and moved early in September '91. Signing a one-year lease would delay my trip to Florida, and any thoughts of returning to California. Although it wasn't intentional, I established roots in Maryland that have lasted to this day.

hapter 7

The Upside Has A Down Side

At twenty-two years old, I was truly living on my own for the first time. I rented that room for a couple of years, living upstairs in a tiny bedroom with the landlord across the hall in the giant master with a loft. An accountant, he was a young guy my age who had bought the house fresh out of college. Smart guy. There was also a bedroom in the basement. Over the two years two different roommates lived there. I quickly discovered that landscaping is seasonal work so when the season ended, I had to find another job. I started working for a moving company, Town & Country Movers. It was tough work! I did that and picked up other jobs too, in order to make sure that my rent was paid on time. As time went on, I was holding down three jobs: Sears Men's Department, my main job during the day, Town & Country Movers, on my days off from Sears, and Roy Rogers fast food in the evenings. It was nice picking up three different checks every week although they were all pretty small. As far as drugs went, I was only smoking weed and drinking on the weekends.

One day when I was off from Sears, and there was no work at Town and Country, I was at home watching daytime tv. I saw a commercial for the Computer Learning Center and I was sold. Computers were the wave of the future and this internet thing was picking up a little steam. I was excited! "Maybe I could have a future after all!" I thought. I took several trains and busses from Gaithersburg to Alexandria, VA to register. In June of 1992, I started going to class five nights a week while holding down three jobs. I met a guy at school who also lived in Gaithersburg and started paying him $20 a week to take me to and from school. Hard to believe now that $20 could fill your car up with gas twice.

My trusty Mustang was constantly breaking down and had become too much to take care of, so I had sold her the previous Spring. With three jobs and school, a brother desperately needed a car. To top things off, I was barely making enough to cover rent and food, so I started scheming for a way to get some cash. I realized that my job at Sears provided the perfect opportunity to make some additional cash on the side. Albeit illegally. I was ringing up a lot of cash sales and if I 'forgot' to give a customer their receipt, I could ring it right back through as a void and pocket the cash. Of course, there were cameras, but I had been there a while and figured security wasn't really watching me, so I gave it a shot.

I started off small with a $40 sale. I kept the cash in my fist and never tore off the receipt; the customer didn't care and walked away. I would then walk to the back of the store and put the cash in my pocket, before returning to my register to void the receipt. This was too easy! Putting the change that I had given the customer back into the register was a little tricky, but I always erred on the side of caution putting a little too much back. It didn't matter because I was still coming away with a profit. I was nervous for the rest of my shift that first time, halfway expecting security to come down and bust me. Even when I left for the day, I was sweating as I walked outside of the mall to the bus stop. The bus took what seemed like forever to arrive. When it finally did, I hopped on, quickly, flashed my pass, and sat down low in the seat peeking out of the window. No one. It worked! Awww shucks; it was on now! I was falling right back into the same pattern: Potential recognized, assistance offered, person (business) taken advantage of, and bridge burned.

When I returned to Sears for my shift the next day, I watched my co-workers carefully to see if they were acting weird. Nope. After a few hours, everything seemed normal. I figured that security wasn't coming down to 'talk' to me. Oh boy! This gave me the greenlight. I tried it again, actually a couple of times that day. Everything went smoothly again. I had my own personal ATM and I was gonna ride it 'till the wheels fell off.

I continued to steal in this manner until I had saved $1,000 and bought an '84 Chevy Celebrity. It had a nice V6 engine and a deep bass sound in the speakers. I was good; no more bus and I could drive myself to school. With my newfound disposable income, I worked up the nerve to ask the manager of the jewelry department out for a date. Her department was right next to the men's department at Sears, and I had been flirting with her for months. However, I knew that being broke didn't make me the most attractive suitor. Having a pocketful of money all the time, gave me new confidence. She was gorgeous: light-skinned and a body that was out of this world! She let me take her to lunch a few times. She never seemed surprised by the fact that I never cared how expensive lunch was or that I seemed to be able to take her to lunch every day. Although my Sears gig was a low-paying job, I explained that I had two other jobs. I guess it made sense to her, so I was good.

One evening, she came over for dinner. I made the only dish I could cook from scratch: Spaghetti with Ragu sauce, garlic bread, and a salad. I even bought a bottle of red wine to go with it. She came over and was impressed with the effort. After we finished eating, she said, "I know red wine goes with spaghetti, but I prefer beer!" She didn't have to tell me twice. I flew to the nearby store and bought a six pack of Coors Lite, her choice. Back then, a fine girl who drank was right down my alley. We both smoked cigarettes too so I thought I'd found my soulmate. After a few beers, we went to my room and fooled around. When we finished, I thought there would be no better way to cap off this perfect evening than to smoke a joint. So, I took one out to the deck and lit up. A few moments later, she came out and sat on my lap. "What are you doing?" she asked. "Smoking a J," I replied. She jumped off my lap suddenly and yelled, "I hate drugs and I'll never date anyone who does them!"

Huh, drugs? What in the twilight zone was going on? This girl drank like a fish, smoked cigarettes like a 1930's movie star but had a problem with weed? My Berkeley way of thinking could not process this. "Weed isn't a drug," I protested, "it's just weed." I didn't want to let her know that I knew what 'real' drugs were, like crack. A no-tolerance policy with that, I could understand, but weed? She was steadfast. Getting dressed quickly, she explained that her brother had gotten hooked on heavy drugs and that it had all started with weed. Apparently, she was very much against any illegal substances. If I had been honest, I would have realized that was my story too. Weed was definitely a gateway drug for me. It took away the mystery and made all drugs ok.

I tell people today that the only drugs I didn't try were the ones I wasn't introduced to. If you had it, I would try it. Period. I was a human garbage can ingesting all kinds of poison and trash. Why? Simply put, that's how I felt about myself. Worthless. Unloved. Disposable. Something that you could throw poison into and it wouldn't matter. Drugs took away that feeling temporarily, but when the effect of drugs wore off, the feeling of worthlessness returned with a vengeance. Pain and misery are what a life of drinking and drugging brings. Although at this point in my life it wasn't so bad, there would eventually come a time, in the near future, when I wished I was dead. Daily. Every day I would wake up with disappointment that I didn't die in my sleep, and I had to face another day of the torture of drug addiction.

"I'll quit!" I cried desperately as she walked out the door. "No, don't quit for me, quit for you," she replied as she got in her car and drove away. I was dumbstruck. How the heck did this happen? One minute I'm on top of the world with the finest girl in Lake Forest Mall. The next I'm alone, abandoned, and rejected yet again. All because of drugs? I looked at the joint, shook my head, and lit it up.

A couple of weeks later, as I was heading to the restroom at Sears, I walked right past one of my co-workers and the head of security whispering together. They saw me and suddenly stopped their conversation, with fake smiles on their faces. Young and dumb, I took no notice and kept it moving. Later that day, I ran my scam, which had become so automatic at this point, I didn't even think about it. As I left for the day, I waved at the jewelry department manager. We were still talking but she kept me at arm's length not really believing that I had quit smoking weed, which of course I had not. As I walked out of Sears and into the main mall, I took two steps and two security guards came up from behind. There was one on each side of me. "James, we need to talk with you. Come with us."

Security caught me red-handed on tape and I quickly confessed to the many other shortages. I was blessed, or cursed I thought back then, with a strong conscience. I always ended up confessing. I was fired and they later pressed charges, although I wouldn't find that out until three years later when I got pulled over in Virginia and a warrant from Maryland popped up. I was also kicked out of the Computer Learning Center around this time. One day after my class was over, I walked into a friend's classroom thinking class was over. The instructor looked up and yelled, "Get out of here!" I took offense and replied with my customary "F*** you!" He took offense, and since there was a classroom full of witnesses, the dean didn't believe my story of responding, "Forget you!"and I was expelled. A couple of months later, I wrote a letter of apology to the instructor, the students, and the school in general. I later apologized publicly and was able to get reinstated. Despite my class now being way ahead of me, I joined a newer class. Honestly, it didn't matter. I was just glad to be back.

After I was fired from Sears, money became really tight. I was still working at Town & Country, but I had let Roy Rogers go since my scam was doing so well. Now I was down to one job, which only gave me work sporadically. This showed me that I was about as high on their priority list as they had been on mine when I was flush. By now, I started coming up short on my rent and my landlord kicked me out. You might think he would have shown me a little grace since I had paid on time for close to two years, but I had also broken his rules by smoking weed in his home. There was also the time that I threatened his cousin who I felt said something slick to me. This didn't give him any reason to have a lot of patience with me and my money woes. Business was business and I was gone.

My friend, Gary, told me about a professor at American University who had a house near the National Cathedral, just above the Georgetown area in Northwest DC. He rented rooms, mostly to AU students, but Gary put in a good word for me and just like that, I was in. By this time, Gary and I had become good friends. Every weekend I took the metro from Gaithersburg to DC, and then when I got my wheels, I drove. We welcomed the weekend the same way every week. Friday night would consist of drinking beer, smoking weed and cigarettes, going to the clubs, getting wasted and sloppily trying to pick up girls, usually without success, and then stumbling back to his apartment. He would pull out the sofa bed for me and I slept there Friday and Saturday nights, going home sometime Sunday evening. During the day on Saturday and Sunday, we nursed hangovers, ate, rode up to Georgia Avenue to cop some weed, and laid around smoking and eating until various friends came over. This was our routine every single weekend for years. Moving to DC within a 20-minute walk and 5-minute drive to Gary made it even more convenient to hang out.

During my first few years on the east coast, I probably smoked crack two or three times. Each time, it was with one of Gary's friends. For some reason it didn't set me off like it did back when I was in California. We also used powder coke when one of his friends had it. Again, it didn't turn me out either. I was pretty content drinking and smoking lots of weed; however, that would eventually change.

I graduated from the Computer Learning Center in the summer of 1994 and was immediately recruited by a company called America Online. Yes, the America Online, or, AOL. At the time, it was a new company on the rise. During the first training session they put the top online companies up on the screen, which were Prodigy, Compuserve, and AOL, in that order. The trainer told us that AOL was rising extremely fast and would overtake those other two by the same time the next year, and he was right. I was hired as a Level I Help Desk Technician, which meant that I was a temporary employee. Within five months, the need was so great that those of us who were still around were put through a three-week training, promoted to Level II, and made full-time, permanent employees. My pay was bumped up from $7/hour to $11/hour with access to unlimited overtime. Today, that doesn't seem like much, but in 1994 my rent was $275 per month, and I had no other responsibilities like a family or car note. Basically, three out of my four weekly checks were disposable income. To top it all off, AOL believed in sharing the wealth. It seemed like every other month they were giving us 50 to 100 shares of AOL stock. I would look at my portfolio and watch my stocks rise, split, and rise again. I couldn't touch my dividends until they vested, which was 1/4 of the total every year until the fourth year when they would fully mature. My family back in California was proud of me; I was actually building a career and a life.

hapter 8

Guess Who's Back?

Everything changed on Christmas Day of 1994. Christmas was always a special day for us when I was growing up and even when we were broke, and Mom was abusing us, she always did her best to make Christmas special. It became a very lonely time for me once I moved out to the east coast. It seems funny that this was the Christmas my life took a turn for the worse. Things were going great at first. I was promoted at AOL in November, I was making good money, and I was talking to a couple of girls. There was nothing serious, but the attention was nice. There was a girl I went to the Computer Learning Center with who always invited me to her apartment during the holidays. She lived with her twin sister and their mom. The twins were around my age, early to mid-20's. They were very pretty but 'big-boned,' the kind of big girls who carried their weight well, and still looked good.

When I pulled up to their apartment complex in Oxon Hill, MD, Toni, my former classmate met me outside. "Hi James!" she exclaimed, always happy to see me and full of positive energy. "Hey Toni! Merry Christmas!" I replied. "You see that limo over there?" she asked. "Yup," I responded trying not to seem impressed. "That's Chuck Brown's limo. He has an apartment over here." "Who's Chuck Brown?" I asked innocently. Toni stared at me as if I were from Mars. "Oh my God! How you don't know who Chuck is? Oh, that's right you from Cali. Well, Chuck Brown is what they call the Godfather of Go-Go. You do know what Go-Go is don't you?" "Yeah," I chuckled. "I'm hip to Go-Go. So, Chuck's the man, huh?" "Uh, yeah!" She laughed as we went inside. "Hey, Ma, James is here! Guess what? He never heard of Chuck Brown!"

I know now how big a cultural faux pas I had made, especially in that area. In Washington DC's Black community, not knowing about Chuck Brown is tantamount to not knowing who the President of the United States is. Unheard of. Go-Go music is as DC as Ben's Chili Bowl and Mumbo Sauce. Heavy on the percussion with lots of call and response, Go-Go is DC to the core. Being from the Bay Area where I was raised on the heavy, simple bass lines of Too Short and a variety of other artists from Santana to Tower of Power to Tony Toni Tone, I hated Go-Go when I first heard it. I just couldn't catch the vibe. The groove was unattainable to my unschooled ear. After I went to my first Go-Go, I understood. You have to go and be immersed in it to get it. The drums, the congas, the guitars, the cowbells, the horns, the singers and rappers, all weave the sounds together to create an experience. The anticipatory energy from the crowd during the slow build up to the moment when the entire band is in the 'pocket,' meaning they catch a groove and ride it in perfect unity for 10 to 20 minutes, is indescribable. There's nothing like it. To this day, I love Go-Go, my favorite bands are Backyard Band, Rare Essence, and Secret Society, to name a few.

So, *I* knew and appreciated Go-Go, but Toni and her family schooled me to Chuck Brown and his many hits, to the point that as I left, I screamed "Wind Me Up Chuck!" to much laughter. We had a great time exchanging gifts, eating an amazing meal, and Toni and I joking and flirting. Her mom made me take three plates home, and I didn't protest one bit.

It was a beautiful, clear, crisp, sunny Christmas day. As I drove home, the laughter and companionship of the afternoon faded, and I started to feel depressed. Another Christmas spent 3,000 miles from home found me dependent on a local family to have mercy and open their home to me-only for me to head back to my lonely room. I thought about stopping by Gary's place, but figured he was with his mom and siblings over in the southeast section of DC. Suddenly, out of nowhere, the thought hit me, Crack. I should get some. No one cares about me anyway, why not? I got money. What's it gonna hurt? After almost three years away from it, aside from a couple of drunk times with Gary's friends, I was nursing the thought of destroying my life. Again. I had moved 3,000 miles from home in the effort to outrun this monster, but it caught up with me that day. In the entire time I had lived on the east coast, I had never thought this seriously about finding some crack on my own. I knew that this was very, very different from someone popping up with some at a party. This was going to be a premeditated mission. Alone. I knew that was how I operated in my addiction: in isolation. To my detriment, I also knew that if I carried this out, I would be back on the road to hell. The road all addicts experience, and once on, it is all but impossible to get off.

I was on my way home driving up Embassy Row on Massachusetts Avenue when I made the U-turn. The symbolism was lost on me that day but today I see it. I was heading in the right direction. Home to safety after a nice day with friends, and I chose to turn 180 degrees to go in the opposite direction from safety to danger. Travelling from health to sickness, and from life to death. I turned around and followed Massachusetts Avenue until it turned into New York Avenue. As I went further east, the neighborhoods started to change. It was 1994, before the gentrification of Washington DC and the make-up of the neighborhoods was well defined. It was very clear when I got to the hood. I made a left on 1st Street NW and slowly crept up the street towards Florida Avenue.

Like I stated before, an addict will find a way. That's how I know this is a disease from which there is no known cure. Through a lifelong program of recovery, it can go into remission. It can even be completely eradicated by the power of God; but simply not using, drinking, shopping, sexing, gambling, etc., doesn't do it. It just lies dormant, ever ready to come back to life once activated. That's why a person in recovery can't play around. Complete abstinence is necessary. One slip and it's off to the races. The disease has been reactivated and studies have shown that it's progressive, meaning that even if you haven't 'used' in 20 or 30 years, it will take very little time for you to be right where you were when you stopped and worse. Personally, I conducted my own research and I am here to report that I have confirmed previous studies: It gets worse, never better, always worse.

Like a true addict, I fell right back into the rhythm of the street. Today, I'm scared to go to the places I went and do the things I did back then. Creeping up 1st St, I turned right on Florida Ave and started a 3-4 square block reconnaissance mission. After about five minutes, I saw my man, a street cat probably in his mid-20's. I drove past him and parked. I got out and walked back towards him. As we came alongside, I said, "What's up, man." He nodded and sized me up right quick. I knew I didn't look like an addict, but I was also a stranger to the hood. In the late 1980's and the 1990's that usually meant one thing- I was looking for some drugs. In Washington DC, the street cats learned quickly that addicts come in all shapes, sizes, colors, and socio-economic backgrounds. Back then, you might sell a dime of crack to a stinking crackhead, turn around and sell an 8-ball, (1/8 of an ounce usually around $125), to a white kid from Virginia, and when you complete that deal one of the Washington-area professional athletes might hit you on your pager with an order. So, some light-skinned square looking dude giving you the look wouldn't faze you.

He looked cool so I asked, "Any rocks out here?" He blinked a little, probably because I used the wrong slang but not by much. If I had requested "stones" or "I'm trying to go uptown," he would've gotten it right away. Coke and crack were 'uptown', and heroin was 'downtown'. "Might be. You ain't the police, is you?" he asked. "Hell naw," I laughed, "just trying to get high man." I guess I passed the muster. "Whatchu looking for?" "I got a hundred," I answered. His eyes lit up and he smiled big. "Wait right here I'll be right back." There's always a great possibility of getting 'beat' during smalltime deals like this but when he left to get it without asking for the money, I was pretty sure I was good. He came back in less than 3 minutes. "Here you go, Slim," he stated. I held out my hand and he dropped 12 tiny bags in my palm. "Two extra, Slim. I be out here all the time holler at me." "Alright, bet," I replied as I handed him the money, and with that our deal was complete. Probably less than 5 minutes from start to finish. Two complete strangers on the streets of Washington

DC, in broad daylight, on Christmas Day 1994. That's how easy it was to score crack in our nation's capital.

Officially back on the crack train. I thought about taking my rocks over to Gary's place and sharing the wealth, but I was never that kind of crackhead. I hated sharing. I took it all to my little room on Garfield St NW, rolled up a piece of tinfoil into the shape of a pipe, sprinkled some cigarette tobacco in, dropped some crack on top, lit up, and I was off to the races for 18 more years of hell.

For a while I kept it somewhat functional. All the newly promoted Tier II reps were assigned the 6pm to 3am shift so that actually cut my using down a lot. AOL tech support was open until midnight on the west coast, but we were the only call center in the country, so that meant working until 3am on the east coast due to the three-hour time difference. I had a couple of buddies who were coming up through the ranks with me named Brian and Andrew, and we would go out to one of our cars when we got off at 3am and smoke a bowl or two of weed. Brian had come up with a 'natural' way to smoke it by fashioning a pipe out of an apple, and this became our nightly routine. By the time we were finished smoking and I drove from Vienna, VA to DC, it was around 4am. It was too late, and I was too tired to creep around looking for 'stones' so I would just go home to bed.

My days off, however, were a different story. I had awakened the beast and it became my priority. Even though I swore off the stuff every time I used it, and promised myself I would never do it again, by the afternoon of my day off I would go out and find some rocks and then buy a pint of whiskey in order to come down from the high and stop 'geeking' when I ran out. I usually stayed up for a night or two and then drank my whiskey, caught a couple hours of sleep, and went to work at 6pm on my next workday. All my other social activities were slowly stopping as smoking crack took precedence. I only had a few friends, and I told them that the overnight shift was kicking my tail and I was sleeping all the time.

I only got ripped off once during that time, but it was scary. I pulled up on a couple of young'uns in that 1st & Florida Ave area. They said they had what I wanted, and I said I had my usual $100. They hopped in my car to make the deal but then another guy appeared, and he hopped in too. At that point I knew I was getting beat for the money I had handed them; it was more a matter of whether or not they would hurt or kill me. It happened every day in DC and I could have easily been another statistic. I looked in the rear-view mirror at the leader directly behind me and he just looked back at me. No one was moving or talking. I almost wanted to say, "Just take it and go!" Finally, they made a move. Two of the young'uns suddenly broke and jumped out of the car leaving the front and back passenger-side doors open. I was thinking, "What took you so long?" Then I noticed the leader was still sitting behind me. I honestly thought he was going to shoot me in the back of my head. Why else would he remain behind? Our eyes met in the mirror again and I swear the look I saw was apologetic. I know it sounds crazy, but I swear he actually looked sorry that they did that to me. It looked like he had seen so much dirt being done in his short life that he was just tired of it. He clearly wasn't worried about getting his cut of the money, because the others were long gone. He just looked at me like he was sorry, shook his head, and quietly slipped out of the car closing his door politely. I closed the other doors and left the area. Now, this is when the insanity of addiction comes into play.

After that experience, most normal people would thank God they were alive and call it a night. Not me! I went directly to the nearest ATM machine, withdrew another $100 and went right back to the exact same spot! There, I copped what I wanted without incident and went back to my room to smoke.

1995 was the best of times and the worst of times. I should have been riding high with a burgeoning career in the new online industry with money coming in, and stock options increasing. My rent was still low, I had no real bills to speak of, and even with my new crack habit, I was still well in the black. Then I met Mary.

hapter 9

Welcome to Life in the Nation's Capital

I used to describe Mary as a white girl with a sister's body. She was a temp at AOL, and I was one of the big men on campus at that point, having been hired permanently. The first time I saw her I knew I was going to go at her. Mary was about 5'4" blond hair, pretty blue eyes, a very shy, coquettish way of looking up at you, a sly grin, and a voluptuous body. I did my usual strategy of completely ignoring her for a while, and then slowly starting to give her a little attention more and more. I had discovered that chat rooms and emails were a great way for me to 'mack' because I could write better than I could talk. I could also edit what I was writing in real time so that it sounded smoother. I met a few girls online like that. So, after we started exchanging pleasantries like 'hi' and 'good morning', I started shooting Mary emails and she responded positively. She had a way of making a guy feel like he was the funniest, smoothest player on earth. It truly fed my ego. I started taking it further and further, bordering on the inappropriate, and she never balked. Finally, I asked her for her number and if she wanted to hang out that weekend. She said, "Sure" so she and her best friend came over to my place. Gary came through and we all went out drinking and carousing in Georgetown. When the night was winding down, we ended up back at my place and I grabbed her and kissed her, which was my go-to move. She was into it and she wanted to spend the night. Gary went home and Mary's friend slept on a sofa in the living room while Mary and I got busy. And that's all it took: I was in love! Again. Once again, I couldn't believe a girl this fine was into me. I kept waiting for the other shoe to drop, and it did, but I was too gone to notice.

As it turned out, Mary was from York, Pennsylvania. She had been in an abusive relationship and she fled to the DC area where she was staying with her best friend, a Black girl with a three-year-old son. In me, I think she saw someone she liked, had money, and would enable her to move out of her friend's home which was getting crowded. I was so gone, if she had said, "Let's get a place on the moon," I would've looked into it.

After about two weeks of hot and heavy romance, Mary dropped the bomb on me. The arrangement with her friend was quickly playing out and with no money or options, she was going to have to move back to York at the end of February. Considering it was already the first week of February and it's the shortest month, this was a catastrophe! Although my drug usage had gone way down since we met, (no crack, lots of weed and beer), my mind wasn't sober. I decided that letting her get away was not an option; she was perfect! So, I looked at Mary and said the four words that I would later regret, "Let's move in together."

Mary looked up at me with what appeared to be genuine surprise. "No, James, I couldn't do that to you. That would totally disrupt your life! Plus, we'd have to find a place, go up to York to get all my stuff, including my dog, and move all in the next three weeks! No, it's ok, I'll just go back to York." There was a flash of a red flag that slowly crossed my mind when she said "my dog" but I quickly wiped it away. "Baby, we love each other, right?" I asked. She nodded, looking like she was close to tears. "We have what everyone is out here searching for, right?" She nodded again and hugged me. "I'm not trying to lose this thing we got," I continued, speaking into her fragrant smelling hair, "So, I want to move in with you, baby. I want us to find a place and do this." "Are you serious, James?" She looked up at me with those doe eyes, "You'd do that for me, baby?" I looked down into her eyes and spoke from the heart, "Of course baby, I love you." "Oh, James I love you too!" she screamed, jumping up into my arms, kissing me. "Wow, I could get used to this every night," I thought. Moving in together seemed like a great idea. To have this voluptuous, beautiful, kind, quiet girl available at all times? A dream come true. Oh, but how mistaken I was.

We immediately started looking for a one-bedroom apartment. Two fools with no credit, no savings, very little tenant history, and two weeks into a relationship that consisted of lots of sex sandwiched between partying and work. Gary told me I was crazy, but I just thought he was hating on a player. As a matter of fact, I thought everyone was jealous of me wherever I went with my fine white girl on my arm. I definitely got evil eyes from the sisters and I just laughed. "I'd be mad too, my sisters," I thought to myself, "Maybe one day you'll have what we have." We found a nice one-bedroom apartment that was actually a duplex. It was like having our own little house, and the rent was only $500 a month. Only one potential problem- it was in the hood.

12th Place and Constitution Ave NE is considered Capitol Hill, but in 1995 it was still the 'hood. It was changing, as our small block consisted of young single black professionals, a white family, some retirees, and us. South and west of us, the neighborhoods got nicer, the closer you got to Lincoln Park to the south and the Capitol to the west. Unfortunately, east and north of us was straight up 'hood. There was an elementary school across the street. I'll never forget hearing the gunshots one night when a young man was gunned down on that playground. He was shot nine times and killed, but that was later on.

Before we could move into our new spot, we had to drive up to York, PA to get Mary's things and her dog. Kevin, a friend of ours from AOL, went with us to help. Kevin and I drove the U-Haul, while Mary led us in her little Chevy Chevelle. When we finally arrived in York, we pulled up to Mary's parents' home. They came outside with no smiles at all. I didn't know them to judge, but based on the angry expressions on their faces, they weren't too happy with their daughter pulling up with two black guys and a U-Haul. Just a guess. Mary quickly showed us what to grab: some bedroom furniture, a sofa, a dresser, and a couple of end tables. She grabbed her dog, a cocker spaniel, and we booked out.

We drove back and moved in the next day. It was the beginning of March, another beautiful cool, crisp day. Kevin helped us again, and we were excited. Being a dog lover, I wasn't concerned about her dog. All animals loved me, right? I had never known a cocker spaniel, and I thought it wasn't very cute, but hey, dogs are dogs, right? I had grown up with Charlie all my life and I loved dogs. Mary explained that she was extremely attached to her dog. He had been hit by a car and almost killed a couple of years earlier and she had nursed him back to health. I noticed that the dog was unusual in that he had no interest in anyone besides Mary. I tried every ploy to get his affection, but he always just turned to her. Hmmmm. "Ok, well, he'll come around," I thought. Then the dog did something I have never seen before or since.

Being in the hood, the tiny backyard was fenced off and had a metal gate. The dog started sniffing around and somehow became stuck in between the steel rails of the gate. I mean really stuck! He started panicking, barking, and whining while trying to squeeze out of the gate. Kevin and I were doubled over laughing at the stupidity of the dog and how absurd it looked caught in the gate. Suddenly Kevin said, "Look, it peed itself!!" So scared was the dog that it had peed right there on the spot and was now not only stuck in the gate but was standing in a tiny puddle of its own pee. This made us laugh even harder as we sauntered over to help the poor mutt. Figuring she was laughing too, I glanced over at Mary, and was met with the iciest stare I have ever received.

The look Mary gave me chilled me to the bone. I had not yet seen this side of her, and I suddenly realized that I had made a huge mistake. Not by laughing at the idiot dog. It was going to be ok, we were going to help it; no, my mistake was hooking up with a young woman who was clearly insane. The saying, "If looks could kill," would be a gross understatement here. The look she gave me said, "I not only want to kill you, but then I want to revive you and kill you again, repeatedly, for laughing at my dog." I know it sounds crazy and far-fetched, but I will never, ever forget that look. It was probably more jarring because it came from such a sweet, innocent face, one that I previously thought wasn't capable even of anger, let alone raw evil.

Kevin saw it too and we both stopped laughing. In fact, we both stopped moving at all as we stared into her face of darkness. Mary killed us for a few seconds longer and then sprinted over to the gate and tried to gently pull the little idiot out. No dice. The thing was stuck good. Kevin and I warily approached, halfway expecting her to hiss like a snake and spit fire at us. We tried pulling, pushing, and squeezing but the dang thing was really stuck. Finally, Kevin said, "Do either of you have a tire jack?" I did, so I ran to get it, anxious to get away from the female Charles Manson and collect my thoughts. "What in the world did I just see?" I asked myself. "I need a freaking joint, man." I always had a stash of weed back then and I couldn't wait to hit it. I didn't want to face any more wrath by delaying the dog's rescue though, so I grabbed the jack and ran back.

We were able to bend the bars the dog was stuck between by turning the jack sideways and cranking it. Pretty ingenious on Kevin's part, actually. The little fool peed a little more as we were cranking, but we didn't laugh this time. When it was freed, Mary picked him up like a baby, cradling him in her arms as she walked into the house. I looked at Kevin and he just shrugged. We didn't even get a thank you. We moved the rest of the stuff in and then Kevin was ready to leave. "Hey, thanks, man," I offered. "No problem, bro! Uh, good luck," he replied, rolling his eyes in Mary's direction. She was sitting on the couch rocking the dog like a baby. "Thanks man," I responded as I walked him to his car. "I'll need it." He laughed as he got in his car and sped off. I turned back to the little row house that was looking more and more like a prison. "What did you get yourself into this time, Jim?" I asked myself. I took a deep breath and went inside.

"So, how's the pooch?" I asked Mary as I walked inside. She looked up at me and smiled, looking like her old, sweet self. "He's fine. Just scared, being in a new place with new people around, and then on top of all that he gets stuck in the gate like that." "I can understand that," I replied as I went to the bedroom and lit up a joint. "I guess we're not gonna talk about the freaking demon that possessed you, huh?" I muttered under my breath.

Later that evening things seemed fine again. We set up the furniture and ate dinner. There was very little closet space which I didn't care about, but Mary had mentioned it before we rented the place. I had overridden her concerns, but now that we were here and I saw how much clothing she had, I realized it was a problem. She didn't really unpack since there was nowhere to put her clothes, but she didn't complain. We figured that we would get another dresser or something. I looked at her and thought that maybe the insanity I thought I had witnessed was an aberration and maybe we would be ok.

That night, episode number two of "James Vs. Mary's Dog" occurred. I had been looking forward to bedtime all night and now it was here. If I had been honest, that was the main reason I made the move- to have sexual access to this fine, innocent-looking, voluptuous white girl on a nightly basis. In our own place? Uh, yeah?! As we laid down, I turned her face to me for a kiss. She seemed a little stiff like there was a little resistance, which I had never experienced with her before. I ignored it and plowed ahead. I'd be doggoned if I wasn't gonna get my "issue" on our first night here. She let me take her clothes off, but I could tell she wasn't all that into it. I didn't really care, though. At that point in my life, other people's feelings weren't much of a concern. Suddenly, as we, well I, started to get really hot and heavy, the dog jumped up on the bed. Now, please understand–I love dogs. Grew up with my best friend, Charlie, and ever since the sixth grade, we also had my stepdad's Golden Retriever, Fraser, in the house too. I absolutely love dogs; however, one rule that was ingrained in me ever since I was three years old was this: No Dogs on The Furniture. Ever. This included: chairs, sofas, tables, and especially beds! I had never had a dog on my bed, so that was shocking even to my marijuana-addled brain. And to make matters worse, when I was trying to get busy?! It was too much. I already had a bit of a resentment towards this dog for not loving me like all dogs do, and for messing up our afternoon earlier. So, I did what my instincts said to do, and I kicked him off the bed.

I believe that was the moment our relationship ended, and I just didn't know it yet. Mary went limp as she let me finish and then she quietly asked, "Did you kick my dog off the bed?" "Naw, I just nudged him a bit and he jumped, crazy dog." Mary looked at me and then went to get the dog. "He always sleeps with me!" she snapped bitterly. She proceeded to take him out to the living room and slept with him on the couch. So much for our honeymoon night in our new place. Mary never slept in the bed with me again. I guess she started plotting her escape then. To be fair, I wasn't very pleasant to live with. Marijuana had a side-effect of making me very moody especially if I wasn't high. I had stopped smoking crack since we started seeing each other, and I wasn't very happy about not having the space and privacy to really get high like I wanted to. I was very irritable and unpleasant to be around. I realized quickly that sex was all we had in common, and we weren't even doing that. Living with another person gets old quickly when you don't have mutual interests and don't actually have conversations. The extent of our communication previously was mostly phone calls to plan when to hook up, having sex, and then going our separate ways. That was over now, and we realized, well she realized, that she didn't really like me all that much especially after I had kicked her dog off the bed.

About two weeks after we moved in together, I received an email at work that read: "James, I can't deal with you and your bad vibes anymore. I've moved out. Let me know when I can come get the rest of my stuff -Mary." I was devastated. I felt like I had been hit with a bat and had my heart ripped out. I started paging her like crazy…No response. I was really going crazy. Where was she? I figured she was with her best friend, so I called her, and she told me Mary wasn't there. I couldn't function. This was not happening! I actually showed my supervisor the email and told him I had to take the rest of the day off. He looked at me like I was joking but saw that I was serious and let me go. I drove home in a daze. I knew things were bad but damn. She's just gonna bounce like that? Where did she go? Who took her in? I sped home halfway expecting her, or at least her dog, to be there. Nothing. Most of her clothes and even some furniture were gone too. Wait, so she had planned this? She waited until I went to work and had someone come help her; who?

I called Kevin and we tried to figure it out. He told me this other guy at AOL was always trying to holler at her even before me and that he was always salty that I had won, so to speak. I had no idea it had even been a competition. I knew the guy, and his name was also Kevin. He was a black dude, kinda dark brown and didn't dress too good. This Kevin was also cool with me though. He always spoke and seemed cool;

him? I didn't know what to think. I kept paging her to no avail. My world was spinning. "This can't be happening."

I called out sick the next day hoping Mary would come back. She didn't and there was still no contact. I couldn't sleep or eat. The next day, I dragged myself to work and sat looking crazy. Suddenly an email came in, and it was her. She was upstairs in her department and wanted to meet outside to smoke a cigarette. Ok, I have a chance! We met outside and Mary wouldn't let me hug her or anything. "Dang," I thought, "Why does she have to look so good?!" She was wearing tight jeans and a form-fitting sweater. I practically begged her for another chance but the look in her eye told me she was already gone. "Wow, she's moved on," I thought, "This dude must have really spit that game."

We decided she would come by that weekend for her things. Devastated, I went over to Gary's place to get drunk and he gave me a piece of advice. "When she comes over, write up an agreement that she'll pay half that rent for the remainder of the lease. Date that joint and have her sign it. Otherwise she's gonna bounce and stick you with the lease without paying a dime." "She wouldn't do that, man," I protested. "Jim don't be a dummy. Do what I tell you. If she's cool like you're thinking she is, then she won't have no problem signing it." "Ok, man. I guess you're right," I replied unenthusiastically.

I went home but I kept drinking. The more I drank, the more I thought I could talk Mary out of it if I just had her in front of me. I knew she was working that evening, so I called her at work. "You're drunk, call me tomorrow," she said coldly and hung up in my face. I called her back. "Look, I just wanna talk to ya," I slurred. "James, I don't want you. I don't want to talk to you, just leave me alone." Click. She hung up again. Oh no she didn't! I called back, "I'm about to come out there real quick so we can talk, baby," I slurred drunkenly. "No, do not come out here, seriously do not." "Whatever, baby I'll see you in a few." This time I hung up with satisfaction. I called Gary and told him I was going out to Vienna to talk to Mary. "Don't do it, man. Just come back over here." "Ok," I lied, "I'm coming." I jumped in my car and drove out to Virginia. Big mistake.

As I pulled into the parking lot at AOL that March evening in 1995, I was rehearsing what my drunk behind was going to say to win her back. Suddenly, before I could even park, I saw flashing lights behind me. What? The cops? She called the cops on me? I pulled over and watched as the officer stepped out of his car and approached. "Step out of the car sir," the officer said as he came up to my window. "What did I do?" I asked as I handed him my license. I knew the cops in Virginia did not play, and this one couldn't have been more stereotypical: White, a little portly, and not smiling at all. He glanced at my license to confirm my name and then repeated, firmly, "Step out of the car **now**." I was scared because: a). I was drunk, and b). his tone was conveying way more of a threat than the usual traffic stop routine. I got out and he quickly spun me around and started frisking me. "What did I do?" I asked again. "Well, James," he began, purposely not addressing me by my last name, "We received a call from a young lady who works here. She described you and this vehicle, and she's scared and feels threatened. Why did you come out here this evening?"

I thought as quickly as my drunken mind could. If I gave him a hard time, he could move on to other things like field sobriety tests. I decided to try the truth. "Sir, Mary is my girlfriend and we're having some problems. I just came out to talk to her. That's it. I guess it was a stupid idea and I'll go on home if that's ok." "Well, I agree with you there, James, it **was** a stupid idea. I'm afraid that I can't let you go home, though because while I was waiting for you, I ran a 50 state check on you and a warrant popped up in Maryland." What the heck? A warrant? "For what?" I asked him. "Looks like a theft charge. Sears? Ring any bells for you, James?" I thought back. Must be some kind of mistake, wait a second, Sears? They put a warrant on me from the 1991 thing? Wow. The next thing I knew, I was cuffed and in the back of the cop car, headed to jail again. This time as the result of petty larceny from years before, all as a result of an alcohol induced decision to try to talk to a girl who had already forgotten about me.

I spent the weekend in Fairfax County jail, and it was a hellhole. At one point, I had to jump up on a table and threaten everybody for some reason. I really don't remember why, but I had been schooled in Santa Rita that in jail, the best defense is a good offense. It was a pure bluff, but I made it out of there unscathed. On Monday, I was extradited to Maryland where the magistrate released me and told me to come back to court on my court date or another warrant would be issued. I called my friend Troy who came and got me from Seven Locks Jail and gave me a ride back to DC. I felt grateful that I had ended up missing only one day of work.

I saw Mary the next day at work and she looked surprised I was still around. She played the innocent role, wide eyes and everything. "I was just scared, James. I thought they would just make you go home, but then I didn't know what to think when I saw your car here and you weren't around. I didn't think they would actually take you to jail!" I realized what a fool I had been, and the spell was broken just like that. When she came over to get the rest of her stuff, the other

Kevin was waiting outside in his truck. I asked her to sign an agreement stating she would pay $1000.00 which was a small fraction of the year-long lease we were in. I wouldn't have gotten a dime if she hadn't signed that. After a month or so, I realized she wasn't trying to give me a cent, so I had her served and we met at small-claims court. We went before a mediator who looked at the signed agreement, then at Mary, then back at the agreement and asked one question, "Is this your signature?" "Yes," she replied reluctantly. "Pay the man," he said and that was that. As we left the court building, the other Kevin was parked and waiting for her outside. "Good luck," I thought. "You'll need it, brother."

To make myself feel better about the whole Mary debacle, I used her money to put a down payment on a new car, a candy-apple red 1991 Mitsubishi Eclipse. It was a very sporty ride at the time. I loved pulling up at work in my fresh ride, especially if Mary and the other Kevin were around. With the new car payment and all of the rent on me, things were pretty tight financially, but it was manageable. Of course, that was until I reignited my relationship with crack.

There is a saying in the 12-step rooms that "Addiction is a feeling disease." Most of us start using because we feel ill at ease in our own skin, and this is universal. This feeling of inadequacy does not discriminate against any background. I always had identity and abandonment issues for obvious reasons, but I'm convinced that even if I had been raised in a family that looked like me, didn't leave or abuse me, and was otherwise healthy emotionally, I still would have been a stomp down addict. I believe this because there just seems to be something in all of us, some dynamic, where we just feel out of place and ill at ease all of the time. Other people may experience these feelings too, but the difference is in how someone who is prone to addiction responds to it. We deal with it insanely.

Sanity is simply "sound thinking" or a "sound mind" and while most "normal" people are able to compartmentalize feelings, talk about them, and 'right-size' them, people who suffer from addiction beat themselves up, magnify the feelings way out of proportion, and attempt to numb them at any cost. Some use drugs and alcohol while others use sex, gambling, shopping, and anything else that will give temporary relief from the constant dis-ease. Since drugs were modeled for me at a young age, that's what I gravitated to, and over the course of the first 40 years of my life, they were my go-to. I always sought an escape, first, as a child, in books and my imagination, then, later, in sports, and finally in the obliteration of consciousness, the oblivion that I found in drugs and alcohol. So, when Mary left me and my world suddenly collapsed, I looked around and realized there were some corner boys right up the street. I never had drugs so conveniently available, so up the street I went.

As I approached the two young guys who were loitering outside of the corner store on 13th and C St NE, I noticed that they were eyeing me suspiciously. I was used to this since I look more like a cop than an addict, so I immediately went into my spiel. "What's up? Any rocks out here?" They looked at me for a second, then one of them spoke up, "You the po-lice?" "Naw, man," I responded, "I know ya'll don't know me from Adam, but I just moved over here right over there on 12th Place." I could literally point to my house from the corner we were on. They questioned me, "You live right there?" I nodded. "Aight, take us over there and your key better work." They served me the stones and the three of us walked up to my door. They watched closely as I unlocked the door and walked inside. I turned around and they were smiling widely. "Ok, you good. Aye we out here all the time. My name Scooby and this is Erk." Ok," I answered, "I'm 'J'." That was it. I was good to go with the neighborhood crew. I didn't know then how deep I would get.

I started using all of the time and it got pretty bad. I fell behind on my rent, but I was able to cash in some AOL stock to catch up. I came to work late all the time, and people started asking me if I was sick or something because I was losing so much weight. My supervisor was super-understanding though and would just ask me to try harder. I promised that I would and continued doing the same.

My next-door neighbor also used. Next to Gary, John was the most highly functioning addict I ever met. He smoked 'Woodies' which was crack sprinkled on weed, in a blunt. John was also mixed and adopted, but he was adopted by well-to-do black people from St. Louis. He came to DC to attend Howard University and ended up staying. A white guy named Mark had taught him the real estate game and John was doing his first house flip when I met him. I watched as he struggled through all the hassles of renovating the house and re-selling it. The process took a lot longer than anticipated, but his parents were supporting him from St. Louis. John never, ever had a 9-5 job, which was something he always bragged about. After about a year or so, he finally completed his first flip. I'll never forget the check he showed me as a result of the flip, because it was $80,000. Had I been sober I would have jumped in that game but I was too far gone by then.

Since I was pretty close to the age of the neighborhood dealers and I had my own place, my house became the unofficial hangout. Most of the guys lived with their mom or grandparents so they would bring their PlayStation over, plug it into my tv, and play video games and smoke weed. They would generally give me a little crack but sometimes they wouldn't. I also was the errand boy going on McDonald's runs for them. I was so eager to be accepted by the 'cool' guys and they played on that. I will say that Scooby and Erk, (whose name was Eric but that's pronounced "Erk" with the DC twang), came the closest to showing me actual friendship but there was only so much respect you can give a crackhead.

The crew didn't actually sling at the corner store where I met them on 13th and C. They had the corner of 12th and D St NE. They were a small crew, but no one really messed with them. Scooby was easily the top producer. He always had good stuff and he never disrespected his customers like other dealers would. Scoob, as he was usually referred, would have been successful in any field he chose. Very intelligent with a magnetic personality, everyone liked Scoob. He and I had many long talks, whenever I wasn't high on crack, and I realized that this kid had more sense than just about anyone that I had ever met. The streets got him though and I don't think he finished high school. He told me once that he had $100,000 saved up and I had no reason to doubt him.

One time, right after they had returned from Atlanta after attending the 1996 Olympic games, he and Erk knocked on my door and rushed inside. Scoob pulled out a pistol and told me to hide it for a while. I was scared even looking at a gun. Erk told him not to let me hold it since I would probably sell it for crack. Scoob just laughed him off and slipped the piece under the cushion of my loveseat. I never even lifted the cushion up to look at it and Scoob came back a few days later and retrieved it. I know it sounds weird but Scoob and I had what I consider a friendship and I was sad to hear in

2005 that he had been shot and killed in the DC streets, after he had turned his life around, obtained his CDL license, and bought his own dump truck.

Another guy I met at that time was Brown Eye. Brown Eye was a wild young-un with a good heart. He would come over when I wasn't smoking and talk with me too. I couldn't believe some of the stories he told me. He liked to rob dealers and then come to our neighborhood and sell off the goods. He always gave you a great deal, I guess because he had no overhead. He did, however, have enemies all over the city. Brown Eye tried to get me off crack by introducing me to his drug of choice: PCP or "Dippers." I tried it for a while and almost went crazy. Some people go on a dipper trip and never return. I remember laying on my bed after smoking a dipper one day and praying to God that I would come back. It took a few hours, but I came back. Once, I drove Brown Eye to Southwest DC to get some dippers. In the car he kept looking around and watching everything. I told him the dippers had him paranoid. He just laughed softly and replied, "'J' I got enemies everywhere." I could tell from his tone that he wasn't exaggerating. A week or so later, he got shot in the face. He somehow survived and was right back to his old tricks. One day, in 1997, I heard Brown Eye got killed. He had run from his enemy and hid under a car, but it didn't work. The killer lit him up right under that car and that's where he was found, dead.

The bully of the block was Whitley. Yes, just like the character Jasmine Guy played on "A Different World." To have such a soft name, Whitley was thorough as hell. Whitley sold weed and crack and the quality of both was terrible. The other dealers who smoked weed would travel all the way to the Orleans neighborhood, (famous for being Rayful Edmonds neighborhood when he was the kingpin of DC in the 80's), to buy decent weed instead of getting it from Whitley who was hustling right beside them. Whitley would bogart sales from the weaker dealers so if you came on the block and Whitley was there, you were pretty much buying from him even though you knew his quality wasn't great. The only one who wouldn't let him take his sales was Scoob. The rest of the weaker guys, like Lips and Black, would just wait around until Whitley left and then pick up sales. Whitley didn't really like me because even though I was a crackhead, I would pull up in a nice car and I lived in a decent place while he clearly had had a very tough life and felt like I was throwing my "success" in his face. I also wouldn't buy his garbage, unless he was the only one on the block. I knew he wanted to hurt me, and I never gave him a good reason to.

One night, Erk called me and asked me to meet him on 12th Street so I could take him home. I said, "ok," because I usually got a dime rock of crack for taking people home. When I got there Whitley, Erk, and another crackhead taxi guy, Jeff were the only ones on the block. It was the end of the night and Jeff was there to take them both home for a dime rock. I was pissed because he was cutting into my "business" but there wasn't much to be done. He owed them money so instead of paying me, they would just take it off of his bill. As we were talking, Erk ran beside the apartment building to hide his bag of rocks in the bushes. Being a crackhead, I watched him closely. I couldn't help it. What I didn't realize was Whitley was watching me. I noted where Erk had stashed his rocks and I tried to act casual while Whitley whispered something to Erk who laughed uncomfortably and glanced at me. That should have tipped me off, but I wasn't thinking straight. They said goodbye and hopped in Jeff's car and as soon as they were out of sight, I made a beeline to the stash spot to take Erk's drugs. I looked and looked but I couldn't find them! I knew I was out of pocket, so I gave up and started walking across the grass back to the sidewalk. Before I could make it, Jeff's car came screaming around the corner, screeching to a stop while Whitley jumped out before it had even fully stopped.

"I got your ass now you red mutha*****!" he screamed. I was terrified. I knew Whitley was a killer and that he had been waiting for an excuse to do me dirty. I looked at Erk who was getting out of the car slowly, reluctantly. Like I said, Erk and Scooby rocked with me. We actually had somewhat of a friendship. But Erk knew I had violated and there was nothing that could be done. Whitely picked up an empty 40-ounce bottle and ran up on me. "Imma f*** your lil' red ass up, nigga! What you doing over there? You snatched Erk's s***?!" I was scared to death, but I tried to think quickly. "Naw man, I just went over there to take a piss. I would never do that man!" I pleaded. This actually gave him pause and I mean he was right up on me screaming so closely that I could feel his hot breath on my face. I was preparing for the blow, but he paused. "Erk, go see if your s*** still there." Erk walked over and picked up his bag. Dang! It was **right** where I had been searching! How did I miss it? Today I think God hid it from me to save me from a bottle to the dome, possible brain damage, or even death. "Naw, we good Whitley. It's here." Whitley looked crestfallen but he wasn't giving up. "Show me where you pissed, J." We all looked at him like he was crazy. "Naw I'm serious, J. Show me where you pissed nigga!" "Man, I don't know where I pissed. You got me so shook man I don't even know!" Whitely looked at Erk. If Erk had nodded, he would have cracked my skull, but Erk shook his head, "Let him go Whitley, he didn't take nothing." Whitley looked at me and then slammed down the bottle right next to me, shattering it on the sidewalk at my feet. "You lucky, J. Next time Imma split your wig, Slim, no bull****!" They jumped in the car and drove off. I breathed. I couldn't believe I was still standing. I cursed Jeff for being their driver and went home.

A few months later, Whitley was killed. Shot in the head in the corner store on 12th and D. We had actually become kind of cool by then. He even allowed me to sell rocks on the block during the brief time I tried to be a hustler. I didn't last long because I couldn't stay clean, but I got a taste of the kind of money you could easily make back then. What an idiot! A kid from the Berkeley Hills hustling on the streets of Washington DC. God really looked out for me, because I could have easily been a statistic many times over. There were many, many people who had a reason to kill Whitley, but we all kind of had an inkling as to who it was. He had clowned one of the weaker dealers and kicked him off the block a couple of days before. The police even questioned that guy, but no one was ever charged with Whitley's murder.

Chapter 10

Something New

I was outside AOL taking a break in the smoking area one day in May of 1996 when my old apple-pipe weed smoking buddy, Brian approached. "Jaaaammmmes, what's up bro?" Brian talked like a surfer from California even though he was from Northern Virginia. He had been in the Marines and had seen some combat in Operation Desert Storm, so he was a little off but really cool and mellow. "What up Brian?" I answered. "Duuude, we went to New York last weekend and we got into something way cool, bro." "Oh yeah, what's that, B?" Brian lowered his voice to a whisper, "Heroin man, we snorted it and it's freakin' amaaaazing dude." "Oh yeah?" I replied. I had never tried heroin before. I was content with my crack, weed, and alcohol, but Brian was persistent. What I thought was just a passing remark was actually turning into a full-court press. "Do you know where to get any, bro?" "No idea, man," I replied. "Well bro, can you find out? I'll definitely make it worth your while, dude."

By this time, I was fully hooked on crack and my time at AOL was drawing quickly to a close. In fact, I was fired a month later for threatening a co-worker. So, when Brian approached me, I figured it might be a good way to make some extra cash for what I wanted. Heroin was unknown to me and I was scared of it. All I thought of when I thought of 'H' was addicts lying in the street nodding with a needle sticking out of their arm. I didn't even know people snorted it, smoked it, and otherwise took 'H'. I had no intention of ever trying it. I was afraid of sticking a needle in my arm or overdosing or something, but I checked around for him.

Unbeknownst to me, at the time, heroin was starting to make a huge comeback in DC. It wasn't at the opioid epidemic stage that we are experiencing now, but it was more prevalent than I thought. Actually, a lot of the dope boys who were slanging drugs were snorting heroin as kind of the new, cool thing to do. Eventually, I found out where to cop it and I started selling it to Brian and his crew at double what I was paying for it. I also found out they smoked crack too, so I doubled up on those sales too. Eventually, after a couple of months, Brian got me to try some heroin and I snorted some. I heard that as long as you didn't do it three days straight, you wouldn't get hooked. The problem was that it was such an effective way to come down off the crack that I started getting some "H" every time I copped some rocks. When this happened three days in a row, I was hooked. Funny, because when I snorted it the first time and woke up the next day without a monkey on my back, I laughed and thought, "I'll never get hooked on that mess. I ain't **that** weak!" Within a month or so, I woke up one day with that monkey sure enough, and I knew the only way to get him off was to sniff some 'H'. I was hooked.

Like I said, I got fired from AOL in June of 1996 when I invited one of the computer nerds outside to fight since he said something slick to me. Instead of coming outside with me, he went directly to report my "invitation." There was a witness who told the truth and that was it. They collected my badge, security walked me to my car, and I was gone. I found out the hard way that in the corporate world you can't play by street rules. The insanity of it all is I knew better, but in my drug-addled mind, I thought I needed to "check" this guy for popping off slick. Total insanity. Plus, I had really bad anger and rage issues dating all the way back to my childhood. Now I was left to wonder, during my long drive from Reston, VA to Northeast Washington DC, after having lost the best job that I ever had: "What am I going to do now? What am I going to do now?"

I soon found that having America Online on my resume was gold. AOL had done a lot of restructuring, including some buyouts, so I would go on interviews and tell them I took a buyout instead of transferring to one of the new call centers in Arizona or Florida. That worked like a charm and I was hired at three different companies, but I never lasted more than a few months. My addiction was too severe by then. The fourth place hired me at the then tidy salary of $38,000 annually, contingent on my passing a drug test. How would I pull this minor miracle off with my growing addiction? The night before the test, I drank about a gallon of a concoction I bought from a health food store, and I went in the next morning to give my sample. They called me a few days later and told me that they were rescinding the offer. The concoction didn't work, and of course I was dirty. That was in May of 1997, and I never worked in the computer industry again.

Right after I was briefly hired at the $38,000 a year job, I went out to California because my mom was giving me her old car. I told the company that I would take the drug screen and start working when I returned. I was able to scrounge up enough money for airfare and flew home to California. I called my old buddy, Carl, as soon as I got home, and we went down to Russell Street. We smoked some crack and then drank a lot of beer to come down. I went home and passed out before 7:00pm on Mom's sofa as we watched a San Francisco Giants game.

The next day, I jumped in Mom's old Mazda for the trek across the country. She actually offered for me to stay and live with her, which I appreciated, but I was anxious to get back to DC and my new job. Back then, I could drive for hours and hours. I drove about 17 hours that first day, which was all the way to Utah, and pulled into a gas station outside of Salt Lake City that night. The plan was to fill up, drive down to the hotel a block away, get a good night's sleep, and then pull out the next morning with a full tank of gas. I filled up and pulled out of the gas station, but the problem was that I forgot to turn my headlights on, and it was nighttime. I made it about a half a block when I saw the flashing lights behind me.

The cop came up to my window and I figured he would understand, so I smiled and told him I had been driving all day, that my mom had just given me this car and I was on my way back to DC. I was tired so I forgot to turn my headlights on, but I was going right there to that hotel. The cop looked at me, looked at my license, saw the name on the registration, (my mom's last name was different than mine), and told me to step out of the car.

Now, I don't scream racism every chance I get, however, I know in my heart that those cops in Utah were racist. No doubt about it. No sooner had I got out of the car when at **least** five more cop cars came screeching up to the set. It was ridiculous; like they had Public Enemy #1 at bay. The issue was that I had left a pack of Zig Zag rolling papers in plain sight, and while that isn't a crime, it was all they needed to go into Dragnet mode. They actually called in a canine unit and had the dog tear through my entire car. They had every door open, including the trunk, with me sitting on the curb in handcuffs. Every car that passed drove by extra slow so they could look at the dangerous criminal on the sidewalk.

After what seemed like an eternity, they realized I was not a drug courier and they huddled up trying to decide what to do with me next. When the first cop approached me, I was prepared to get the cuffs taken off and get my ticket. Instead he grabbed me by the arm and started walking me to his car. "I'm taking you in. Your driver's license is suspended," he announced. "Wait. What?" I protested. "Suspended for what? I haven't even been driving! I haven't had a car to drive! What is it suspended for?" "I'm not privy to all that information, sir. All I know is that Washington DC has suspended your license, you're driving a car that isn't yours, and I'm taking you to jail." Just like that, and that was it. He took me to jail somewhere in Utah and they towed Mom's car. I got in touch with her that night and she bailed me out. It didn't stop her from being **very** angry with me. She didn't believe me when I told her that I was being railroaded and that my license wasn't suspended.

I was able to get my car out the next morning, but only after the towing company finally reached my mom at work and confirmed I had permission to drive her car. I drove the rest of the way across the country worried that I would get pulled over again and thrown in jail. Fortunately, I made it back to DC safely. As luck would have it, about two weeks later, I **was** pulled over for rolling through a stop sign in

Georgetown. The officer was really nice, and I told him I thought my license might be suspended. He went back to his car, ran my license and came back. I expected him to throw the cuffs on me, but instead he told me there was absolutely nothing wrong with my license. It wasn't suspended and he let me off with a warning about the stop sign. The cops in Utah had straight up lied about my license. Eventually, I was able to repay my mom the money she had paid for my bail in Utah. I probably could have sued for false imprisonment, but I didn't have the stamina or attention span to take it that far. I was too focused on my next high.

By now, I was hooked on heroin and crack. The sum total of my life was that I was a 29-year-old drug addict. After blowing the last computer industry opportunity, I worked a few different low-paying jobs around the city. After a while, the Mazda got booted and towed because I never paid my tickets. I became a bicycle delivery person, delivering pizzas for Dominos and lunches for a company called Steakaround to businesspeople around the K Street corridor. My heroin habit was getting bad and I was quickly getting to the point where I needed it in order to function. I wasn't making enough money to support my habit and I was getting desperate.

One evening, when I was delivering pizzas, I stopped by the dope spot on 9th and O Street NW. The guy I thought was selling me dope suddenly pulled out a huge knife and took my money and my bicycle. I was terrified and gave it up with no resistance. Later, when my dope habit got really bad, I remembered how scared I was when I got robbed and figured I could scare people just as easily to get money for dope. So that's what I did; I started robbing people.

This is the insanity of addiction. A kid from the Berkeley Hills, robbing people and doing drugs in the streets of Washington DC. There's a saying in the recovery community, "Yale to Jail." The meaning is two-fold. The obvious interpretation is that once addicted, it doesn't matter what accomplishments or status you have achieved, it can all fit inside a shot glass, crack pipe, or syringe. It can also fit on a credit card for the shopaholics, a bed for the sexaholics, and a pair of dice for the gamblers. It also means the disease of addiction doesn't discriminate. It doesn't care about your upbringing, socio-economic background, education, etc. Some of those environmental factors may have bearing, regarding access to substances and methodology of usage, but at the end of the day, unchecked, addiction will ruin your life.

Now that I'm sober, I look back on my life of addiction and thank God for looking out for me. The "Yale to Jail" saying is funny because one of my neighbors, actually the kid who grew up on the other side of the fence from me, actually went to Yale! All of the neighborhood kids my age grew up to have very successful careers, and from what I can tell, full and productive lives; and then there's me. At that point in October of 1998, I was 29 years old and a full-blown drug addict, sleeping on Gary's sofa and delivering sandwiches on a borrowed bicycle.

My heroin habit was getting worse and worse, and by that time I was snorting it daily. I had just enough of a habit to make me uncomfortable- not quite physically sick, but uncomfortable knowing I needed a "one and one" (a snort for each nostril). I was at work one afternoon at the sandwich delivery job. It was slow that day and I was feeling desperate because I wasn't making enough in tips to slide off and pick up some dope. Standing around in the kitchen waiting for a delivery run, I saw a large pair of scissors which triggered the memory of being robbed at knifepoint. I took the scissors and left work. My plan was to go and rob someone, which was something I hadn't done since that drunken night with Stone eight years earlier. I didn't rob anyone that day. I just couldn't bring myself to do it, but a couple of nights later, on Halloween, I did. I took a portable CD player from a woman. She actually laughed at me at first thinking I was joking so I tried to snatch it, and after a brief tug-of-war, she let it go shaking her head at me. That was the one and only time I robbed a woman. I traded it for a dime bag of heroin to get the monkey off my back.

My career as an armed robber lasted about two months and I could have starred in the show "World's Dumbest Criminals." I always went to the Capitol Hill area in DC and I never wore a mask. If a victim told me he wasn't giving me anything, I would plead and tell him that I was sick and needed it for drugs. If he still resisted, I would apologize and leave. I never had any weapon other than a pair of scissors or a broken bottle, which I would try to wave around menacingly. Once, I was rummaging through a victim's backpack and found a bunch of prescription pills, an addict's dream. My question to him: "Do you need these to live?" He looked at me in disbelief and said, "Uh yes, I really do." I gave him his bag back and ran off. I found out later that he told all of this to the police when he made his report and the judge took it into account when she sentenced me.

One morning, a couple of days after Christmas of 1998, I was a few blocks east of Union Station looking for a victim. It was around 7:30am and I had been up all night. I was totally out of place, looking like a crackhead amongst a sea of professionals who were suited and booted on their way to Union

Station or the Capitol Building. I saw a little guy walking alone who looked like he wouldn't put up any fight. I learned that people never interfered when someone was being robbed so I didn't care about all the potential witnesses; I was tired though. So bone-weary and wrung out from the drug abuse and lifestyle that I couldn't move. My mind was telling me to cross the street and get him, but my body wouldn't respond. I just stood there leaning on my get-away bicycle watching helplessly as my victim sauntered past.

I looked up a while later and noticed there was a police car on the next block with two cops inside watching me. I knew they were wondering what someone like me was doing here at that time of the morning. I admit, I looked like I was up to no good. I saw them and I knew I needed to make a run for it, but again I was tired. I just couldn't move. They drove up slowly and parked in front of me. They got out and started questioning me. Apparently, the Capitol Hill Neighborhood Association had grown tired of my shenanigans and had gotten the United States Capitol Police involved. They had a bunch of reports of robbery, and I fit the description. They asked me to empty my pockets and discovered that I had a broken bottle on me. I told them it was for my protection. I thought I was talking my way out of it, I really did. As I was talking, though, I looked up and noticed that one of my previous victims was walking down the street on his way to work. I tried to hide my face, but he saw me and ran up to the officers screaming, "That's the mother*****r who robbed me!" At that point the jig was up. I was cuffed, thrown in the police car, and taken to jail. My overwhelming emotion? Relief. Again, the insanity of addiction. Life is so rough that you're relieved when you're hauled off to jail.

Chapter 11

Back to a Familiar Home

1901 D St SE is an infamous address known to Washingtonians–the DC Jail. Now I was **really** scared. Probably the only thing worse than going to jail is going to jail with a dope habit. As I went through the booking process at the local precinct and was then shipped over to the jail, I could feel the familiar pangs of the beginnings of withdrawal. I knew I would be extremely uncomfortable soon. My heroin habit rarely got to the point of throwing up, sweating, and shaking, but I would definitely be ill. No energy, no appetite, very achy like the flu. Processing new prisoners takes a long time, and as we went through the process at DC Jail, I knew I would need help. I told the first nurse that I saw that I was a heroin addict, and I told her loudly. I didn't care who heard me! She gave me some ibuprofen and said I would begin receiving medication to help with withdrawals within a day or two. A day or two? I wanted to throw the useless pills back at her, but I went ahead and took them, almost regurgitating the water I drank to wash them down.

I was assigned a housing unit and went to my cell. The next 24 hours were pretty rough, and I didn't get out of my bunk except for chow where I ate a tiny portion and dragged myself back to bed. The next night I received the magical pills and they held me together until I had "kicked." After a few days, I was weak, but the habit was off my back. Good thing because the magical pills stopped coming too. I finally had the strength to wander out into the pod and start getting used to my new environment.

Like Santa Rita, DC Jail was segregated and the different races cliqued up together. Unlike Santa Rita, there were **very** few whites, so they didn't make up enough to even have a group. The pod was 80-85% Black, 10-15% Latino and the rest was a smattering of White, Asian, and Middle Eastern. As usual, I made friends with everybody, but I had to be on my toes and not break any unwritten laws of which there were many. My race-jumping was tolerated as long as it was clear that my loyalty was to the blacks, which was not a problem. Actually, everybody pretty much got along as long as the other races stayed humble and in their place, which they did out of survival instinct. It's pitiful that jail is one of the few places in America where black people have power, and trust and believe that black folks run DC Jail.

In many ways, I learned how to be a man in jail. By that I mean I was taught various things that I just never paid attention to before and I notice now in society that a lot of people haven't been taught these things. In jail, the slightest slip-up can be taken as a show of disrespect and must be rectified immediately, or your life could hang in the balance. If people in the free world cultivated the sensitivity toward other people that it takes to survive in jail, I believe society would be more civilized. I know that sounds paradoxical, but it's true. For example, if you so much as brush against someone, just the sleeve of your shirt barely touching the sleeve of the other man, you better darn well notice it and say, "Excuse me." If you don't, your disrespect will either be called out on the spot, "Damn, Slim, you can't say excuse me?" Or, it will be noted and rectified later. In that case you could very well be killed or jumped, ending up in the infirmary trying to figure out why. To this day, I remain hyper-sensitive to my physical proximity to other people and my internal alarms go off whenever someone enters my "zone." I have to consciously tell myself almost daily that the person who is standing **right** behind me in line, or walking **right** behind me in the grocery store, or bumps into me without a word probably doesn't realize that what they're doing is offensive. I also realize that many people are raised in societies where there is no such thing as personal space because of overcrowding. Trust me, all of this goes through my mind in an instant as I mentally combat the instincts ingrained by five years of living in a state of hyper-sensitivity.

It's amazing what a human being can adapt to as a result of living in a 6'x9' jail cell with another human. As long as people are warehoused like this, let's not pretend that jail is meant to be rehabilitative, it's purely punitive; there's no way you can cage people up like animals and then expect them not to behave like one upon release. People argue that convicts were behaving like animals before they were locked up so they should be treated as such upon incarceration. If that's your stance, I hope none of your loved ones ever make a mistake or a bad decision that gets them locked up, because you will change your tune quickly. Factor in, too, that the majority of men and women in city or county jail haven't even been convicted of a crime. They are there because they have been **accused** of a crime, but due to the economic incongruence of the bail system, their families can't afford the bond to get them out. They languish in jail awaiting trial while their families suffer in their absence. Since they're locked up and can't go to work, the first thing they lose is their job. Consider, too, that they can't see their spouses or children except through a dirty plexiglass screen or on video calls, so they begin to spiral into hopelessness and despair.

There is no kindness in jail, no friends, no safety, and nowhere to let down your guard and just 'be.' That's why so many people take plea-bargains. At least they're getting out, at least they can hold their spouses and hug their children; however, they end up with a permanent criminal record which makes it hard to gain employment. This ultimately results in the cycle being perpetuated all over again. The American jail system is a multi-billion-dollar industry which deals in human capital and is set up in such a way that it is extremely difficult to escape the cycle once caught up in it. If you have the resources to get bail and pay an attorney, you can probably avoid these kinds of consequences; but for the rest of us, a slip-up can devastate an entire family.

Not to say that my story is an example of a "slip-up." I definitely deserved what I got; however, many lives are ruined due to the harshness of the American justice system which penalizes first and sorts it out later. Many an innocent person, usually of color, has taken a plea bargain in order to get back to their family only to be haunted by their criminal record for the rest of their lives. Many a person, again, usually of color, has been sentenced under harsh guidelines and received tremendously long prison sentences for nonviolent offenses only to emerge 20-30 years later into a world that has left them behind. They are left with an, at times indifferent, parole officer and no system of support in place. The powers that be understand this and bank on that man or woman committing another crime or parole violation and going back to prison. I beat the odds by completing my sentence and my time on parole and I know others who have done the same, but it is extremely difficult to achieve. Once "justice involved," it is difficult to emerge clear of any restrictions. Modern Day Slavery is an accurate description. Bail was set for me and I don't even remember how much it was. It didn't matter, I knew I wasn't going to bail out and I would either take my case all the way to trial or accept the plea deal.

Seared in my memory is the day my public defender visited me with the plea deal. The D.A. was offering thirty years to life. Either accept that plea or take the felonies they were charging me with to trial. I knew that if I was found guilty, the judge would throw the book at me for wasting everyone's time, and taxpayer's money, by taking the proceedings all the way to a jury trial. I cussed my public defender and went back to my cage. Thirty years to life! What do you even do with that? My mind refused to process that new reality.

Before I was locked up, I had taken to visiting different churches. Something was drawing me to them. Even high or on my way to get high, I would stop at a bible study or some other service and check it out. I didn't know what was really going on and I didn't understand much, I just knew I was being drawn and that people were receiving **something** from these places and had been for centuries. I always believed there was a God, a "Great Designer" of everything. It seemed foolish to think the intricacies of science and creation weren't the result of a master plan of some sort and were instead just the result of a random **bang** after which everything just fell into place. I didn't argue that there was probably a **bang**, however it just seemed obvious that it was a planned **bang** with well-thought out results. I also had this notion that Someone was watching over me, I just didn't know how to communicate with or just what to do with this Someone.

When I arrived at DC Jail, and took stock of my surroundings, I noticed that there were different religious factions. Well, there were two: The Christians and the Muslims. Being a spiritual "free agent" having been raised in neither, I gave both a good look. The Muslims were followers of Islam and their group was attractive because they were clearly looking out for each other. It was obvious that if you joined the Muslims, you were automatically protected. They also helped their new members by giving them snacks and cosmetics, which they made a big show of doing. This was very attractive to someone like me who was broke with no outside support. I honestly was very close to joining them. But I didn't. I just couldn't shake the feeling that joining them was more like joining a gang then worshipping God.

The Muslims in my pod were very aggressive and clearly proud of the intimidating energy that they operated out of. I learned later that they really weren't practicing true Islam, which is a religion of peace; but I didn't know any better at the time and figured if I wanted to roll like that, I could join an actual gang and not have to pray five times a day. Speaking of which, it struck an off note with me that, although they prayed "religiously" five times a day every day at the same time, they always repeated the exact same prayer every time. That just seemed disingenuous. I mean, how can you pray the exact same memorized words five times every day and be sincere? Is that what God wants to hear? The exact same words repeated five times a day every day by everybody? Is that what a Father desires to hear from his children: daily memorized repetitions? Maybe, if I had joined them and really dug into their doctrine, it would have made sense, but I was turned off.

The Christians, on the other hand, weren't very intimidating at all. Joining them would not have the added benefit of protection and if they gave new people anything, they were doing it in secret. I liked what they were doing though. I was fortunate that in the pod I was housed in, the Christians were pretty bold. They gathered every night in the lower level of the pod, where they fellowshipped, sang worship songs, and prayed. I noticed this and thought it was good. They just seemed very sincere in not praying rote prayers, but really passionately crying out to God in prayer for each other, their families, even the correctional officers, and other inmates. After a couple of weeks, I wandered down and joined their circle.

I started going to the circle every night, admittedly because I was facing thirty years to life in prison. It was hard to wrap my head around the fact that this was my reality. Thirty years to life. How had I ended up here? I wanted to explain to the authorities that this wasn't really me. That the animal they thought they had rightfully put in a cage was just a scared mixed-race kid from the Berkeley Hills. That I had caught some bad breaks, gotten introduced to crack and heroin, and it had all turned me into someone else. I wanted to explain that I knew what I must look like on paper but that if you just had a conversation with me and heard my story, you'd realize that I needed help, not a cage. I looked at the correctional officer's (CO's) faces for some hint of sympathy or understanding and was met with blank or angry stares. Surely, they could look at me and tell I didn't belong here. If I could just get the right person to listen, they would let me out, and this nightmare would be over.

But I did belong there. I alone had chosen to use the very drugs that changed my behavior so drastically. I had behaved like an animal, invading other people's space and destroying their sense of safety. All for a temporary high that would wear off and have me back on the streets acting like a predator. When I look back, I can see how my whole life had led up to that point and that I was a perfect candidate to go down a road like this. I had no sense of self, no sense of identity, no sense of safety or security. Having been abused, ridiculed, torn down and never built up; of course I sought relief! But at the end of the day, no one forced me to do anything. All the decisions were mine and now I had to pay up. Thirty years to life.

I enjoyed the prayer circle. There was a sense of fellowship and I even started clapping and trying to sing along with the songs. I tried reading my bible, but it didn't make much sense to me. It just seemed like old stories from ancient times, but there was something there. Every time I read about this Jesus and the way he healed and forgave and seemed to go right to the heart of every question that was asked of him, I felt calm. I liked that he wasn't all uptight and religious, and that he hung out with sinners and the people the religious Pharisees shunned. I read about his first miracle of turning water into wine. Ok, Jesus! Definitely a cool dude. One evening, I hit the buzzer in my cage when they called for chapel service. They popped my cell door and I lined up with the others to go to chapel.

I went to the chapel service consistently after that first time. I wasn't sure about the whole 'church thing' but I kept coming back. The preacher was a CO who worked at the prison in Lorton, Virginia where they housed the DC guys once they got their sentences. He voluntarily came to DC Jail and preached on his own time. At first, I didn't know what to make of him because I had never experienced a preacher live and in person. The guy was like someone you'd see on tv. He had a Jherri Curl, and the sweat and curl grease was flying everywhere. He'd be all excited, running around, sweating, curl juice flying, and just preaching hard! "HA! You **must** get saved, HA! God can turn, HA! your life around, HA!" I sat in the back laughing at the preacher with the collar of my orange jumpsuit turned up because I had to maintain my image. I'm sitting in jail facing thirty to life with D.O.C. (Department of Corrections) printed on the back of my jumpsuit and I'm worried about my image? Remember Step Two? Insanity.

One evening, I sat in chapel service laughing at the preacher, ready to make my mind up that it was all fake; all this Christianity stuff was bull. It was just a way to get on tv and make money off of people. I had to admit though, this guy seemed sincere. I couldn't figure out what his angle might be, and I concluded that he legitimately believed what he was preaching. I mean this brother preached **hard** and with a lot of passion. I could tell he really believed that Jesus could change our hearts. I was sitting back watching the show when all of a sudden he shouted the words I'll never forget, "Ya'll doin all this robbin, HA! Killin, HA! Fightin, HA! But you not **man** enough, HA! I said you not **man** enough, HA! to stand up and give God praise!" My ears perked up. My mind raced, "What'd he say? Not **man** enough? Wait a minute bro, don't come for my manliness now! You're messing with my image." I sat up straighter as he continued and it seemed like I was the only one in the room and he was preaching right at me, "Some of ya'll facing a **lot** of time! Give Him praise, HA! Some of ya'll mad at God! Give Him praise! HA! I dare you to stand up and give God praise, HA! Watch what he'll do in your life, HA! I dare you, HA! I said I dare you, HA! If you say you a man, stand up, HA! Stand up, HA! Give Him praise! HA! This ain't for punks, HA! This Christian walk ain't for no suckas, HA! I dare you, HA! This Christian walk ain't for no sissies, HA! I dare you! Wait a minute, HA! I double-dog dare you, HA! I said I double-dog dare you! Stand up, HA!!! Praise Him, HA!

I was compelled. My mind was racing, "Dang it, **I** am facing thirty years to life. Maybe God **can** help? Maybe I should try it?" I stood up hesitatingly feeling like a fool but desperate enough to try. The preacher saw me, "That's right, brother! Don't worry, HA! Who's on your right, HA! Or who's on your left, HA! This is between you, HA! And God, HA!" I stood all the way up and started trying to lift up a praise, "Hallelujah," I muttered. "That's right brother!" He urged, "Lift up those hands! Surrender to God! Tell Jesus thank you!" I raised my hands and closed my eyes, "Thank you, Jesus," I said, slowly at first, "Thank you, Jesus, Hallelujah, Thank you, Jesus." "That's right, brothers," the preacher continued, and now there were a few others trying it. "He suffered for you! HA! He died for you! HA! He rose for you! He's seated at the right hand of the Father right now, HA! Interceding for you! HA!!! He LOVES you, HA! Praise Him, men! Praise Him!" With that, I let out a shout, "Thank you Jesus!" and something happened. The only way I can describe it is it felt like something in my spirit shifted and clicked right into place. It was like a back alignment for my soul. I didn't even realize I was out of alignment, but I actually **felt** it. I believe there is something in all of us that yearns to worship God. We usually misdirect it and worship other people or things like money, our job, etc. But when we line that thing up and direct it toward our Creator, something happens. I'll never forget that evening in February of 1999 in DC Jail. I went down front and said a prayer with the preacher and he told me my soul was saved, but this was just the beginning of my walk with Jesus. He told me to put on my seatbelt and be prepared for the ride of my life. I didn't realize it then, but oh how right he was.

I went back to my cage that evening, got down on my knees and really prayed for the first time in my life. "God, if you're really there, I don't really know what I'm doing right now and I'm sure I'm not doing it right, but I just want to say, I'm sorry for what I've done. I know I've made a huge mess of my life and I've done some terrible things, but could you please forgive me, Lord? Please just forgive me. I'm so sorry for what I've done, I'm just sorry."

I trailed off, kneeling there in my cell with my head bowed, tears streaming down my face. I just kept shaking my head and saying, "I'm sorry, I'm so sorry, God, I'm sorry" As I was kneeling there in my cage, shaking my head, crying, and saying "I'm sorry," I started to feel something comfort me like a warm blanket was being wrapped around my shoulders. To this day, the best way I can describe what happened next was that I **felt** His voice. I didn't hear audible words, but I felt them as sure as if He were speaking directly into my ear and the message I kept hearing was, "Trust Me." God communicated to me that I had done everything they were charging me with and more, and it was time to trust him and stop leaning on my own understanding; my own strategies, my own schemes.

Here I was, thirty years old, sitting in jail facing thirty years to life. That was the sum of my life to that point. 3,000 miles from home and family, no friends to speak of, and even if they were to release me that day, nowhere to go. Oh, and I was a stomp-down drug addict with $3.00 on my books. That was the sum total of my life to that point. "Yale to jail." From the Berkeley Hills to a cage in the bowels of the Washington DC Jail, and all I heard God saying was, "Trust me."

God made it very clear that trusting him meant taking the deal. I impishly asked if there was anyone else up there that I could talk to, but He seemed to ignore that. "You did everything they're charging you with and more so admit it and trust me for the outcome. Your best shot has landed you here, so give me a shot. Trust me Son, trust me." His "voice" was so still and soft, yet so compelling. I knew He was right. I mean, I **knew** in my soul that He was right. Every fiber of my being knew that He was giving me my answer, yet my human logic rebelled. No one in their right mind would take thirty years to life. Facing that kind of time, you might as well take your chances and go to trial. But I had to admit, nothing I did had ever worked. Here I was at thirty years old, in a cell, and I knew He was right. "Trust me," He said, "Trust me." "Ok, God," I finally responded, "I'm gonna do what you're saying, I can't believe I'm saying this, but I'm gonna trust you, God. But if this doesn't work, if I get all this time, I'm done with you God. I can do bad on my own!" I fell silent and just knelt there with my head bowed. I had an image of God smiling and nodding His head in approval. I felt peace.

I got in touch with my public defender and told her that I wanted to take the plea deal. There were a few seconds of silence over the phone, but she recovered enough to respond, "Ok, you want to, ok, well Mr. LeBlanc that is commendable, um, but I would advise you that the judge can choose to give you the entirety of the sentence or she can show leniency which they sometimes do when you take the plea.

Judge Krone is tough on violent offenders, but she's fair, too. I would advise you to try to get as many people as you can to write character letters to the judge. Ask family, friends, clergy, anyone who can vouch for your good character to send her the letters. I am pushing for a split sentence where you do a little time in jail, and then enter long-term drug rehabilitation since that would actually address the issue. So, I will come get your signature and submit the acceptance of the plea offer. In the meantime, I need you to get the letters and we'll take it from there." We said our goodbyes and hung up. I sat in the pod playing cards with some other inmates, not daring to divulge that I had accepted a plea offer for so much time.

Chapter 12

A Time of Reckoning

Sentencing Day is always on a Friday. I was awakened earlier than usual, around 4am, so they could get everyone down to the bullpen where we would be handcuffed, shackled, and loaded onto the jail bus for the ride to court. Even though we were in chains and on a jail bus, traveling the few miles from the jail to the court building on Indiana Avenue gave us a sense of freedom. We were out in civilization and not within the confines of the jail. We saw people outside living their lives and I yearned for that. Just to experience the normal, mundane life of a free man. Able to go outside whenever I wanted, able to go to a job, come home, eat what I wanted, kick back on the sofa or Lay-Z-Boy and flip on the big screen. Able to sleep in a comfortable bed and take a shower in total privacy. Able to love, laugh, and live. Just a normal life. Man, that sounded so good right about then.

We saw beautiful women walking or driving to work and we yelled our undying love and commitment to them through the closed, locked windows. We saw street-smart kids stop and stare at the "Bluebird" jail bus with different expressions; some aloof, some fearful and some with respect.

I wondered which ones would take that ride one day. Some of the older guys looked at the bus and nodded. Maybe they'd taken the ride before? Others would yell and wave, even yelling people's names who they apparently thought might be on the bus. Most of the general public didn't even notice us or understand who was on the bus. Why would they? Today, I notice prison busses all the time. It's hard to tell if they have passengers since the windows are blackened, but I try to give a little nod or a raised fist. It's amazing what those gestures of encouragement mean to the men and women who are taking that ride, especially on a Friday.

We drove down the ramp into the bowels of the court building where they unloaded us and put us on an elevator, ten at a time. When we arrived at the main floor, we were herded into another bullpen, the door was slammed behind us, and a heavy silence fell amongst the group. Slowly, with nervous energy, conversation began building among the men. I was asked what kind of case I was working with. "Armed Robbery, Judge Krone," I replied. All other conversations tapered off and everyone looked up. "Krone?" my questioner echoed, "**And** you got a violent crime? Aw wow, Slim, you know they call her the Hanging Judge, right?" I was actually unaware of this tidbit of information and would have been glad to have never been enlightened to such. That kicked off a rollicking conversation in which the guys told Judge Krone stories, most of which, I hoped, were fiction. It turned out most of us were seeing her and the other guys were facing their upcoming sentencing with what had to be a false bravado. One guy stated, "Aw man, Krone be giving out football numbers, Cuz! I know I'm gone!" 'Football numbers' meant that she always gave out double digit years, usually in the wide receiver category of 80-89. I tried to laugh it off but now I was really scared. I had accepted a plea of thirty to life and judging from this new information, that was probably exactly what I was going to get.

I wondered how long I was going to have to wait in the bullpen since it was a one-person-at-a time process. The first guy was led out and he came back pretty quickly, within 10 minutes. He was immediately peppered with questions, "How she acting, Slim?" She in a good mood?" What's it looking like today?" He sat down and smiled wryly, "The DA asked for a continuance so I gotta go back in a month." That didn't help us at all. We still didn't know what kind of numbers the judge was giving out. "LeBlanc!" Suddenly, the deputy was at the door demanding my presence. I was next. "Good luck, Slim!" "Yeah, you'll need it!" came the cries from the bullpen as I was led across the hall and into the courtroom.

The sterility of the courtroom was shocking to my senses. After the last few months of living in a dark, dirty dungeon, the courtroom was incredibly bright and clean. Everything looked like it was in perfect order, as if my mere presence, handcuffed, chained, and in a rumpled jumpsuit was disturbing to the environment. I wanted to let everyone know that despite my appearance, I liked cleanliness. I noticed there were quite a few people in the gallery, probably family members of my crew back in the bullpen. I was led to the table where my lawyer gave me a weak smile. I looked across at the DA at the other table and he looked angry. Then, I finally looked up at the judge.

I expected to see an old, bitter, gray-haired, mean-looking woman looking down her glasses at me with a frown. I was met with a youngish, maybe mid-forties, attractive woman with brown hair looking down her glasses at me with a neutral expression. Judge Krone seemed to look at me for a few ticks past comfortable, like she was sizing me up. I knew my mom had written her a letter; I just didn't know what she said in it. Whatever it was, I suspected it had an impact on the judge, because my mom was a great writer.

Judge Krone confirmed with both counsels that a plea agreement had been reached, and then she asked the DA for his recommendation. He ticked off all the counts against me and highlighted the impact statements from the victims. He conceded that I showed a modicum of decency when I asked the one victim if he needed his pills to live, but he concluded that I wasn't fit for society and should be locked away for as much of the plea deal as possible. He clearly would not have been upset if she gave me the whole thirty years. She asked me if I would like to make a statement before she passed sentence. I stood up and said that I was very sorry for what I had done. I said that there was no excuse, because even though I committed the crimes in desperation to get drugs, it had been my choice to start doing drugs in the first place. I asked for the mercy of the court and to be sent to rehab.

Then Judge Krone spoke, "Mr. LeBlanc, what you have done to your life is a family tragedy," she began. "Wow," I thought, "Mom must've pulled no punches." "You have ruined your life," she continued, "I agree that you need drug rehabilitation, however I have victims here who are afraid to leave their homes because of the trauma you inflicted on them, so prison is where I am sending you." "I'm outta here," I thought, "Football numbers and I deserve them." Judge Krone paused and looked at her paperwork as if considering something she had written down. To this day, I believe she had written a sentence on my paperwork, probably the night before, to guide her at this moment but something was giving her pause or maybe it was Someone. She stared at her notes and appeared to scratch something out and write something else. She was still frowning, though and I feared the worst. How could I have been so stupid to take that deal? I could have at least fought it out at trial! Where was God now? I was completely at the mercy of the judge, totally helpless. My legs were shaking, and I couldn't swallow. She looked up.

"Mr. LeBlanc, I have to say, however, that I **believe** you when you say that you're sorry." I looked at her and I saw an openness to her expression. I felt a lightness start to overcome my spirit and a heaviness that I didn't even know was there started to lift. God was doing something again, something I had nothing to do with, and I was just along for the ride. "Only someone who is truly remorseful would take **that** deal," she continued, "and I believe you should have another chance. Now, like I stated, you **are** going to prison, but not for thirty years. On count A, your sentence is two to six years. On Count B, your sentence is one to three years to run consecutively. This means, Mr. LeBlanc, that your sentence in totality is three to nine years. You will be eligible for parole in three years. Do **NOT** blow this chance, Mr. LeBlanc, it's the only one I'm giving you." My knees buckled with relief and I managed to squeak out, "Thank you." She allowed herself a half-smile and busied herself with paperwork as I was led out of the courtroom and back to the bullpen.

It may sound funny, but I was floating as I walked, shackled, to the bullpen! I had expected to get at least ten years and I was walking out of there with three. As I was let back into the cage, I thought that I was wearing a stone-face, but the guys saw my glee immediately. "Ok, I see you're smiling, Slim! What she give you? What you working with?" "Three to Nine," I replied with a smile. My response was met with shouts of joy, "Oh wow, she in a good mood today!" "Ok, let me go get my time!" "Nobody better not go in there and piss her off!" I sat back with a smile. A smile only someone walking into a courtroom facing thirty years to life and walking out with three to nine would know about.

About a month later, I was shipped off to prison. That was in 1999 when the facility in Lorton, VA. was closing, and all the DC inmates began to be shipped all over the country. It was, and still is, a horrible time. Washington DC inmates are scattered all over the United States in federal penitentiaries and private prisons. Because of the distances separating them, it is nearly impossible for their families to visit and for their children to know them. I saw so many human rights violations that it became commonplace. Very few of us even thought along the lines of what our rights were. We subconsciously concluded that we conceded them when we were convicted, but in hindsight, we were treated like animals, herded from one corral to the next. Human beings being treated like slabs of beef, each slab worth $40,000 a year to the institution holding them as a commodity. Prison is **big business**. Big business, and we added to the ranks by believing that our lives weren't worth valuing. So, we made decisions that led us here to the cages of the United States penal system; a system that didn't care about us and made clear that our rehabilitation was an afterthought. I think the worst thing I witnessed, and I saw a lot, were the times a father and son were locked up in the same institution together, sometimes in the same cell. An illustration of the master plan working to perfection, and a people falling for it generation after generation.

I was shipped first to Occoquan which was near the facility at Lorton. When I went through R & D, Receiving and Departure, I saw a fine woman inmate working behind the counter where they gave out the clothes. I muttered out loud, "Wow, they got females here?" An older inmate looked at me and said, "That ain't no female, Slim, that's a 'boy'." That was the beginning of my prison education. The two rules I was schooled to early were: Mind Your Business and Don't Get Involved with "Boys." There were guys in there who had been taking hormone pills and were actually shaped like women, the slang term for them was 'boy'. At first glance you would not know it was a man. I found out during my incarceration that rape wasn't happening much anymore in prison, at least not the ones I was in. There were enough willing homosexuals who actually looked like women that if that was your thing, there was no need to take it violently. The danger was in getting involved with someone else's "girlfriend." I witnessed a few stabbings over "boys." Thank God I didn't swing that way, so I easily avoided that kind of drama.

I was only at Occoquan for three days when they put me on a bus to Lorton. I was glad to leave, because it was a dangerous place. My second day there, the medivac helicopter had to come land in the yard to take a stabbing victim off to the hospital and I was told that was a common occurrence. The guys on the bus were happy to be going to Lorton or "The Hill'" as it was referred to. Lorton was a legendary place to Washingtonians. Going to Lorton was a rite of passage back in the 1970's and '80's, and it was so lax back then that for the street guys, it was like a vacation. Lorton was closing down when I got there. I was on one of the last loads and DC inmates were being shipped all over the federal system in 1999. When I got off the bus, I went through R & D and then to my dorm. I was pretty scared when I got there. I had heard of Lorton and when I arrived, I could tell there were guys there who had been there for many, many years. I really didn't know what to expect. Would I have to fight? Would I get stabbed? Raped? I mentally prepared myself for anything and vowed to fight as hard as I could if need be.

Nothing like that happened at all. Everyone was pretty laid back and just doing their time. Being on the yard at Lorton was almost like being on the streets. There was drugs, alcohol, and actual real money being handed back and forth. Like any other jail, I found that if I minded my business and didn't look scared, no one really bothered me. I played some basketball and although I'm no MJ, I was good enough to get some respect. Just like anywhere, respect in jail is earned and it's given if you're actually good at something and not just a talker. In fact, I met some of the smartest, most talented guys I ever knew in prison.

I was at Lorton until June of 1999 and then I was shipped off to Sussex II in Virginia. That place was a nightmare. We pulled up on the bus and immediately these two huge drill sergeant types ran on the bus screaming at us, "You Mother******s aren't in DC anymore! The party's over ladies!" Clearly, they were trying to establish authority. As we walked off the bus another huge redneck was right there barely containing the biggest, ugliest, growling, snarling Rottweiler dog I have ever seen. I can't lie, it was intimidating. We went inside and were immediately led to our pods with the drill sergeant-types screaming at us, "Do you see these lines, ladies? They are different colors for a freaking reason! **Do not** cross the red line! If you do, look up there at the control bubble ladies. Do you see the officer with the shotgun? Good! Cross the red line and you **will** be shot. Those are rubber bullets, girls, so they won't kill your sorry asses but they will sting!" A few months later a guy got stabbed in the neck while at a table playing cards in the pod and the officer shot that gun. I can't explain how loud that gunshot was in that pod, but the noise alone almost gave me a heart attack.

I was in Sussex II for about a year and it was bad. We were locked in our cells for 23 hours a day with one hour "rec time." The only thing that saved my sanity was the job I was given as a teacher's aide in the school, so I was out all morning, actually being treated like a human being by the teacher I worked for, Ms. Marlowe. She looked and sounded just like Aunt Bea from the Andy Griffith Show, and she was a very sweet lady. She treated every man there like a valuable human being and we all appreciated her for that.

After about a year, we were shipped off to Youngstown, Ohio, which was a 450-mile, eight-hour bus ride cuffed and in chains. We were there for six months or so and then shipped back to Sussex II. I got my old job back in the school and settled back into the routine. One day, in September of 2001, we had just started our day at school when we were abruptly sent back to our pods. Rumors were flying that something big had happened like America had been bombed or something. We were in our cells and the trustees who were cleaning the pods and could see the TVs started reporting that some airplanes had hit the World Trade Center, both towers! Someone asked a trustee what it looked like and he walked past the cell shaking his head and muttering, "It looks bad, Slim, it looks bad." When a hardened criminal is shaken up by an event, you know it's serious. We later found out that the Pentagon had been hit too and that a teacher's aide in another class had lost his mother in that one. She was killed at work in the Pentagon.

I did the last six months of my time in an actual federal penitentiary in Lewisburg, PA. Going to the "feds" was like going to heaven for those of us who had been in the hellholes of Sussex II and CCA of Ohio. The first time I went to the chow hall, the guys I was with just watched my reaction. I just stood there with my mouth and eyes wide open. I could not believe the amount of food they were giving us; it was literally all you could eat. They had organized softball and basketball leagues, and different kinds of activities including bible study and church services which I participated in eagerly. I even became an usher in the church there.

I was so hungry for the Lord that I even went to the Spanish services! I didn't understand much but I loved how they really reverenced the Lord. The language of worship is universal. I appreciated the outside guests who came in and held church services. I respected that they came in knowing they wouldn't receive anything from us. That's one of the reasons I minister in places like jails and homeless shelters today. I remember how much it meant to me when I was in those places. I studied the bible and grew in my faith. Although it was good for me, it was still prison.

I saw a lot of things there: drugs, fights, and stabbings. I never used drugs while in prison, because I didn't want to be known for any form of weakness. That conscious decision making showed me that I could be clean if I wanted it badly enough. Like I said, it's amazing what a human being can adapt to. I adapted to living in a 6'x 9' cage with another grown man. I adapted to smelling all the odors we shared with each other, and I adapted to hanging a sheet up in the middle of the cell so I could have "privacy" while using the toilet. I adapted to not encroaching on the other man's carefully carved out space in the cage. If I was walking to the toilet and accidentally kicked one of his shoes, since our shoes were lined up on the wall opposite the bunk bed, I apologized and straightened it. I learned that you tear off a piece of toilet paper **before** you pee so that when you finish, you wipe off the toilet seat whether you sprinkled a little pee on it or not. I had a lot of cellmates, some good, some bad. My favorite celly was Jim-Jim who I met after I was sentenced and sent to prison.

Jim-Jim was in his mid-forties when I met him during my second year of incarceration. He had been locked up since the 1970s for murder when he was 18 years old in a case of, "We're from beefing neighborhoods, and we both have guns so it's going to be you or me." Five foot ten inches, barrel-chested, and strong, Jim-Jim was the funniest person I have ever met or heard. He had me laughing so hard I could barely breathe with tears running down my face as I begged him to shut up. He also taught me how to box. The deal was, I help him with his reading and writing and in return he teaches me how to fight and how to do my time. He literally taught me as if I were eight years old stepping into a boxing gym for the first time. How to step, breathe, and punch. He admonished me to tuck my chin, keep my left up to protect it, and keep my mouth closed. A jaw is easier to break when one's mouth is open. We wrapped my hands in strips of sheets, and he put flip-flops on his hands to catch the punches like a trainer. He would tell me what to throw: "Jab, double that jab, uppercut, uppercut to the body, overhand right!" He taught me what became my favorite four-punch combination: a left-right one-two followed by a left uppercut and an overhand right. Devastating! We had to stop with the flip flops when my last overhand right hit his hand and popped his elbow out of place. He laughed it off, thank God, and relegated me to shadowboxing until he healed up and we started using a rolled-up mattress like a heavy bag.

He also taught me how to really work out. Jim-Jim's back arms, his triceps in particular, were so hard from decades of push-ups, that poking them was like poking a wall or metal table. One time he made a muscle and turned the back of his arm toward me saying, "Poke that back arm." I could not believe how hard it was. No give at all. Literally like tapping on a piece of metal. I could imagine the power one of his punches had with that back arm behind it. We started doing 1000 pushups a day of all different kinds. He taught me the importance of stretching and calisthenics. There were just lots of things regarding exercise that I never knew or paid attention to.

Jim-Jim and the DC guys from the 1970s came of age at the old Lorton prison and they were real gangsters. They didn't act tough; they were tough and didn't have to prove it. It was obvious. Guys like Jim-Jim, Lightning, Blango, B.H., (who was around 50 years old and cut up like a 24-year-old bodybuilder but died when we were all at Sussex II from hepatitis and lack of medical attention), were older G's that took a liking to me because I respected them, listened to their wisdom and learned how to 'bid.' They had been locked up so long that they knew how to do the time and not let the time do them. I learned everything I could from them once I got my sentence and started doing my time. Without their tutelage, I don't know if I would have made it. At the very least, they helped the time go way smoother than if I hadn't met them.

I ended up serving four years straight. I was denied parole my first time up, which was January of 2002, but they gave me a release date of June 2003. From that point on, I knew when I was being released. I was actually let out of Lewisburg in February of 2003 to serve the last four months in Hope

Village halfway house in Southeast DC. That would be followed by four years of parole. I said my goodbyes and walked through the gate, escorted by a guard whose parting words to me were, "I hope I never see you again!" "Me too!" I replied.

Chapter 13

The Sweet Taste of Freedom

When I boarded the Greyhound bus in Pennsylvania that chilly February morning in 2003, I was shocked; **everyone** had a cellphone! I couldn't believe it when I saw little kids talking on their phones. Cell phones were just coming to be a thing when I "went away" in late 1998. Now, a little over four years later, they were everywhere! I contemplated that and wondered what else had changed in the world as the bus rolled towards DC. I thought about my future and how I was going to stay clean, too. I knew I could do it. I didn't touch any of the plentiful substances available in prison and I felt great! But as we drew closer and closer to DC, I felt that old familiar tug and it scared me.

A major part of the addiction experience is the anticipation and the actual act of "copping," followed by the rush of getting away with something. There is a heightened sense of anticipation once you have the substance in your possession and are on your way to go use. The times I cared the least about anything or anyone else in the world wasn't when I was actually getting high; it was when I had just copped and was on my way home or to an abandoned building or wherever. **Nothing** else mattered. It's part of the insanity of the disease, or dis-ease, of addiction. It completely takes over your thinking and you obey with no questions asked. Even knowing what the end result is going to be: heartbreak, bankruptcy, desolation, hopelessness. It simply doesn't matter. The only thing that matters is getting that first hit, snort, drink, or injection up in you, consequences be damned. I know it's a disease that centers in the mind because most addicts are otherwise extremely intelligent, strong, capable people who can exhibit great strength of will in every other aspect of their lives. But when it comes to mood-altering substances, the insanity of the first drink, hit, snort, purchase, snack, card game, sexual encounter, takes hold and there's no escape. Very few of us actually have the spiritual awakening or complete psychic change it takes to recover. For those like me, it takes a spiritual maintenance program, practiced daily to the best of our ability, in order to stay clean or recovered. It takes work to stay clean, but boy is it worth it. If you're reading this and you're in the throes of addiction, you can recover. Just give yourself a chance, take wisdom from those who have gone before you, and don't quit before the miracle!

I didn't know all that on the bus ride back to DC. All I knew was that the closer we got, the more of a tug I felt to go cop. It had been over four years since I last touched a drink or a drug, but it didn't matter. I wanted to get high. Now. We disembarked at the Greyhound station on 1st & K St NE and I knew I could walk up to 6th & L NE and cop in less than 10 minutes. I also knew they would probably give me a drug screen when I got to Hope Village and that made my decision all too clear. I had just enough sanity left to decide not to blow it on my first day back. Many people do, though. I hopped in a cab and told him to take me to "The Lane."

Nicknamed "Hopeless Village" by 100% of us who have ever resided there, Hope Village is located across the street from the notorious Woodland Terrace projects on Langston Lane SE, one of the deadliest areas of Washington DC. Does it seem logical to put a place designed to help you to make a successful transition back into society in the heart of crime and devastation? That's what happens, though because if you try to put a halfway house in a nicer neighborhood, the residents will be outraged for the sake of public safety and the threat of derailed property values. It is for this reason, as illogical as it seems, that halfway houses are always placed in the worst neighborhoods. Residents will still protest, but it falls on deaf ears. Getting off the bus on Alabama Ave and walking down Ainger Place and Langston Lane everyday felt like an exercise in survival, yet I did what I had to do.

The halfway house was set up in four brick buildings. Each building had a bunch of two to three bedroom 'apartments' with each room housing two men. There was a shared bathroom and a living room with a sofa, a couple of chairs, and a coffee table. The unit I was put in actually had a tv in the living room, because one of the guys had an extra one. Actually, after living in a two-man cell for the last four years, it looked pretty good to me. Still, with four grown men in a small space, things got tight pretty quickly so I started signing out to look for a job immediately.

Guys were always coming "home" talking about who was hiring, so I was able to land a job pretty quickly. In 2003 jobs were plentiful if you wanted to work. I'd been working all my life and was no stranger to hard work. We heard that a construction company was hiring, so one of my roommates and

I took the one-hour, two-bus-and-a-walk trip to Hyattsville, MD to apply. We were hired on the spot. I learned all about underground construction which basically meant: Dig a trench, lay some pipe, cover the trench, and go home filthy. I did that for a little over six months. Up every day at 4:25am, walk down to the chow hall building and eat a Hope Village breakfast, grab a Hope Village bag lunch, and run up to the bus stop on Alabama Ave to catch the 4:55 W4 to Deanwood Metro Station. Then we jumped on the R12 which dropped us off right in front of Burger Delite on Kenilworth Ave in Hyattsville. From there we walked up the hill to the yard, jumped in the compressor truck, and went to the day's job. Some guys brought a change of clothes since they knew they'd be really dirty by the end of the day, but I didn't bother. I wasn't going anywhere but back to the halfway house after work and I didn't care what the people on the bus thought about me. Sometimes the school kids would "jone" on me about my clothes and how dirty I was, but that rarely happened. A black man in his 30's on those bus routes looking like he had a dirty job was pretty common.

Hope Village performed random drug screens and it seemed like my name **always** came up for screening. That's one of the main reasons I stayed clean. There was plenty of opportunity to use, though. The neighborhood crew sold crack right across the street from the halfway house and if that wasn't bad enough, one of my roommates who was from the Sarsum Corda projects in NW started selling crack. It was clearly all he knew to do. He had been 'home' less than a week when he came in one day all grins, "Hey 'J' I'm back on, Slim!!! I'm 'bout to be paid!" He reached down in his pants and pulled out a bag full of smaller baggies which all contained "dime" rocks. My stomach flipped and I hoped he didn't notice. He was probably testing me to see if I was a crackhead, but I played it off as well as I could and didn't bite. It would have been disastrous if I became known as a crackhead in Hope Village, and I knew that I would have a one-way ticket back to prison due to dirty drug screens.

In June, I was released from Hope Village and went to live with Gary, who had purchased a condo in SE off of Minnesota Avenue near Orr Elementary School. He had a pull-out sofa that I slept on until December when I moved into my own spot. By then I was working with another company doing utility locating which was much cleaner and I got to take the company truck home. The place I moved into was way across town on 14th and Decatur St NW right next to a metro bus barn, which kept me up all hours of the night. I rented a room in a single-family home with other renters. Our landlord was a cab driver from Ethiopia who lived elsewhere with his family. The day I moved in, I walked into my own room and just lay on the bed thanking God. 2003 was about to turn into 2004 and things were looking up.

During my stay at Hope Village, I started visiting a small storefront church whose pastor was the mother of one of my Christian brothers in the Penitentiary. Pastor North was one of the kindest, loving, godly people I have ever known. Her son gave me her number before I left, and I reluctantly called her one day. She invited me over to her home which was a couple of blocks away from the church and I went over the next day. When I arrived at her beautiful home on 16th and Massachusetts Ave SE, I realized it was three blocks from DC Jail. I walked up the stairs past the well-kept lawn and rang the doorbell. I felt really vulnerable not being used to reaching out yet knowing that I needed some kind of spiritual support and guidance if I was really going to make a go at this new life. To my relief, Pastor North swung open the door and gave me that huge smile and a great big-ole hug. Instant acceptance, no questions asked. She was just a woman who was always guided by the Spirit of God and the love that abides there.

Pastor North was probably in her late 60's back then and she became somewhat of a surrogate mother to me. She even said I looked like I could be one of hers. She had eight grown children and they were all college graduates. I was locked up with the one who had gone astray. He was one of my best friends in prison as neither of us looked like we were supposed to be there. I started going to her church whenever I could. It was really small, usually just a few family members, but I received support and godly love. I went to the Bible Studies, too, which one of her son's taught. I was also staying clean, seeing my parole officer once a week and giving drug screens.

Pastor North's church had a nice bedroom upstairs above the sanctuary which was a tiny living room with three rows of chairs. In June of 2004, her youngest son got married and moved out of that bedroom so she asked me if I wouldn't mind living there. She would charge me way below market rent which was good for me, and she would have someone present at the church most of the time which was good for her. I said "Yes," immediately because the house I was living in had become infested with bedbugs and I had just gotten into a knock-down drag-out fight with the guy who brought them in. In addition to me, my landlord was also renting out the basement to this guy I'll call "Mike" who had a dirty rottweiler and a mangy, decrepit cat. Everything was fine because the basement was totally separate from the rest of the house, so we never saw Mike and his weird zoo. Unfortunately, he started coming up short on his rent. He turned out to be an alcoholic as well. To solve the problem of his not paying rent, the landlord moved him and his motley crew into the main house, specifically the room right next to mine. Mike, who was 6'7" but **really** skinny, his dirty dog, and his little matted up cat all moved into a little bedroom. We quickly found out that he had other pets too, the bed bugs, which quickly spread to our mattresses as well.

Bed bugs are horrible. I've lived in jails, homeless shelters, and trap houses but that was the **only** time that I experienced bedbugs. They wait until you're good and asleep and then they creep out from the mattress and start feasting on your blood. I would wake up at 2 or 3am and be so desperate that I would jump in the truck and go to the 24-hour CVS to buy all manner of bug spray and repellent. I sprayed everything down, but nothing worked. They were indestructible. Whenever I pulled one off my skin and squashed it, my own blood would squirt out of the thing. We complained to the landlord, yet he did nothing. Mike had been living there for almost 10 years, so he was a fixture. I was getting really irritable from lack of sleep and I started having words with Mike who liked to argue in the hallway with his Rottweiler by his side. Finally, one day, it happened.

I was eating lunch on a Wednesday afternoon when Mike came home and started talking mess. I confronted him the night before and kind of punked him a little, so I guess it had been eating at him all day. He came home looking for a fight. We had words and it started getting heated. One of our other roommates was there too, but that was no help because he was the house tough guy and neither Mike nor I wanted to look weak in front of him. Finally, Mike invited me outside to throw down and I jumped up like it was the best idea I'd ever heard.

As I followed him outside, I tried to remember all the cool stuff Jim-Jim had taught me. I also thought about just jumping on him from behind, I mean all's fair in a street fight, right? As we were walking around the side of the house and I was playing out so many different scenarios in my mind, Mike turned suddenly and punched me dead in my eye. I thought that I was a safe distance away but being so tall he reached me with ease. I guess he thought I would go down, or fold up or something, because he just stood there and looked at me like he had done the most. Big mistake. I ran at him throwing everything I had and then some. It worked, too. I was touching him up pretty good and all he could do was clinch. I took that time to catch my breath and I relaxed a little. Big mistake. Mike broke the clinch, reared back, and punched me in the exact same eye again! Our roommate was sitting on the bench on the front porch and he was instigating big time, "Ooohhhh, awwwwww, ouch!!!" That set me off again, so I commenced to beating the crap out of Mike. He kept trying to clinch but I wasn't going for that anymore and I pushed him off and literally beat him to his knees. He was kneeling there, grabbing at my shirt which had ripped, and I stood over him feeling powerful as heck. Our roommate was standing on the porch now yelling, "Knock him out James! Finish him!" But I couldn't do it. He was done.

I looked up and realized we were now in the front of the house which faced busy 14th street and there were lots of people in cars watching us. Being on parole, I didn't want any drama with the law, so I pushed him off me and he fell to the lawn. I'm not gonna lie, beating Mike up felt great. But when I went to the mirror and looked at my eye, I realized that he might have lost the fight, but the two punches Mike landed were very strategically placed. As light as I am, I was going to have a black eye for a month.

So, when Pastor North called a week later, I was ecstatic. "Yes, I would be happy to move into the church!" I packed my stuff, praying no bed bugs came along, worked it out with the landlord who was very understanding, and I was gone. I moved into the spacious upstairs bedroom of the storefront church in June of 2004. It was on 15th & Independence Ave SE. I realized that it was less than a mile from my old place on 12th Place NE, but I wasn't concerned. I had been clean for 6 ½ years, 1 ½ of those as a free man on the street. I was good, right?

Chapter 14

Which Way Do I Go?

I was 35 years old and had never felt whole and complete. By August, I started feeling the old itch to find my biological family. Even with my burgeoning faith and sobriety, I knew there was a hole in my soul that would never feel filled until I knew who I came from. Even Pastor North, whose solution for all things was Jesus, Jesus, and more Jesus, understood this yearning. I started praying not even to physically meet my biological family, but just to somehow find a picture of an actual blood relative. Having no children of my own, I had never met anyone with whom I shared the same blood, at least not knowingly. I realized that being sober, I was feeling everything I had always pushed down with drugs and alcohol. Praying helped, talking to Pastor helped, but nothing was going to scratch that itch except knowing who I "belonged" to. I never lied to myself about that. I would tell people, "Yes, I have tools to help me cope, and I know God is my eternal father; but I just want to see, even if just a picture, someone I'm related to. I think I would be more comfortable in my own skin if I knew who else had this blood flowing in them. Why do I have this nose? What characteristics do I share with whom? Are there any medical issues that I should know about? Who am I?!

Taking action was all that was left to do at this point. I was able to connect with a woman named Judy who had an organization in San Diego that helped adoptees find their birth families. We started corresponding and I sent her all of the vital information that I had like my date of birth, name of the hospital I was born in, etc. The adoption agency that handled my adoption was a private one, so both sides had to sign releases for identifying information to be shared. I signed on my end, but no one from my biological family had ever signed. Since that didn't pan out, it was on to plan B. Judy looked up all of the births at the hospital that I was born at, on my birthday. This gave us a promising lead, as she was able to come up with nine groups of names, which included the mother and father's last names and the baby's birth name. I was one of those babies! Even knowing that tiny clue to my identity helped to fill a small part of the gaping hole in my soul. I was one of those babies, but which one? The internet hadn't evolved into the super sleuthing resource that it is now, so I would need to hire a private detective to take a deep dive into these people's lives, past and present. Since I couldn't afford that, I thanked Judy and gave up. Again.

Feeling defeated, empty, and depressed, with no real support to maintain my sobriety, I made a disastrous decision. Getting high had been in the back of my mind since my release from prison a year and a half earlier and I decided it was time to use. Self-pity and resentment were the new culprits this time, because I was reliving the same sting of rejection that I always felt. Except now, it was reignited by the fact that I made some progress but would never uncover the truth about my biological family. Life wasn't fair and I wanted to check out for a while. Where did I go to scratch that itch? A guy that I met at Hope Village. He lived about a five-minute walk away and I knew his uncle, who lived with him, used drugs. I had been over there a couple of times before just talking, joking around, and watching sports on tv. Today, I was there for something completely different, and I had my story ready. I told them I had a girl at the house who wanted some dope (heroin) and some stones (crack). The uncle left and came back with just what I needed in 10 minutes. I thanked them and went home, where I threw away my hard-earned years of sobriety. I sniffed dope and smoked crack for the first time in over six years and it was like I'd never stopped. I was back on the train. Again.

I was able to hold it together for about a year and a half, but by the end of 2005, I was really struggling. I had gone back to the underground construction job and I was using drugs regularly. I had given my P.O. some dirty drug screens, so I was now being sanctioned to go down there twice a week, on Tuesdays and Thursdays. I knew it took a solid three days, four to be safe, for the drugs to clear my system. In my mind, this gave me a small window of opportunity to use on Thursdays immediately after I peed in the cup. I could use all the way until Friday morning and then have a solid four days to clean up before giving my next sample. This all seems rational in the mind of an addict. How can I beat the system, get high, and stay out of jail? And that is exactly what I did.

My strategy wasn't too complicated. I would buy the drugs on Wednesday night, keep them overnight without touching them, drive to the PO's office on Thursday morning with the drugs in the car, drop my sample, and then go outside and use the drugs right there in my car in the parking lot. Boy, did I feel like I was beating the system on those mornings! I smoked and snorted all day on Thursdays, even at work. It was nothing for me to stay up all night, finish up early Friday morning, and go to work Friday on no sleep. Insanity. I slipped a couple of times and let the using bleed into Friday and even Saturday. When that happened, I drank gallons of water and prayed I gave them a clean sample. Every now and then I would come up dirty, enough to keep me on two-a week drug screens, but infrequent enough to keep them from locking me up. Since I couldn't use every day, I was able to stay current on my rent and even buy a car, a 1999 BMW 318I two-door hatchback. I told myself I was functional and that I had figured out how to use and still succeed.

I kept that routine going until January of 2006 when it all came crashing down. I went to one of those tax places that file your taxes and give you your refund on the spot. Now what would happen by giving an addict $4,000 at one time? My "strategy" of using within a certain window of time went right out the window! I went on a week-long binge with my tax refund. Although my strategy was abandoned, I knew that I still had to "pay the piper" when I went to see my PO. He was ready to violate my parole when I went to see him, so I begged him to let me go to a rehab. He eventually relented so I took a leave of absence from my job to enter a 28-day program in Virginia. I was 37 years old and in rehab. Again.

I was seriously starting to think that this might just be my lot in life. All kinds of potential wasted on never being able to stay clean. I just couldn't shake the feeling that I wasn't worth it. Nothing had occurred in my life to change the narrative that I had decided was mine: I was damaged goods because I was discarded at birth. The labels "unwanted" and "unneeded" suited me. Anyone who has been put up for adoption can relate. It's extremely difficult to come to terms with, and it would take me years to figure out.

I got through rehab and was determined to stay clean. I even asked Pastor North to go into the trunk of my car and get rid of the drugs I had stashed there. I knew that if the crack and heroin were in my car when I got back home, I would use; no doubt about it. If that were to happen and my subsequent drug test would be positive, I was guaranteed a trip back to jail. Washington DC was now under federal guidelines which meant that if you violated parole and were sent back to jail, every day you had been on the street was forfeited and you had to start your parole time all over again. At that point I had about three years on the street and a year to go. If I was violated, I would have to start over and stay trouble-free for four years once re-paroled. It was March of 2006 and I was due to finish my entire sentence in April of 2007. Just a little over a year left to go. Any sane person would do what they had to do, but somehow, I knew I wasn't going to make it.

I had met a white dude in rehab named Ben. He was a loud braggart who had a lot of money and let everyone know it. Being a bit conniving myself, I cut into his social circle and we became cool. I didn't know how that would benefit me immediately, but I was doing what I knew to do, and that was playing an angle that might pay off.

Ben contacted me when he got out of rehab about a week after me. I had been going to 12-step meetings and I even had a sponsor who was starting to meet with me as we began to develop the trust that it takes to begin to work through the 12 steps. I was back at work and was very happy with the girlfriend who had waited for me to get out of rehab. She was a church girl who had never used a drug in her life. Things were looking up, until Ben called.

"Hey man! I just got outta rehab! Let's grab a steak!" It sounded good to me, so I asked where he wanted to meet. His answer surprised me a bit, but I shrugged it off as Ben being Ben. He wanted to meet at one of the high-end, "classy" "Gentlemen's" clubs in Georgetown. I didn't have much of an issue about going to a strip club, as I had frequented them here and there for years. But I never thought of eating dinner in one! Even though I was "saved," and I knew Jesus as my Savior, I definitely knew how to sin better than I knew how to live righteously. Off to the strip club I went.

It's funny how things change once you have an experience with the Lord. I believe the Holy Spirit comes in and indwells the Believer. Even though my natural inclination was to head towards sin, I stopped feeling comfortable in it almost immediately. I felt different when I walked into the strip club that night. In the past, all I saw was naked, or near naked, women dancing and smiling, booze flowing, and everyone seemingly having a great time. Now, it was like I had a new set of eyes. I saw beyond the surface into what was really going on. I saw that these women were being manipulated and used, and the customers were really empty souls searching for some kind of fulfillment. It didn't matter if it was the false smile and insincere attention of an attractive woman. I saw the filth, degradation, and ugliness just under the surface of this "classy" establishment. I didn't get any satisfaction or sense of moral superiority from this, however. I actually **wanted** to feel fine in the strip club. All I knew were places like this, the underworld, places of "ill-repute." This is where people like me went! If an unwanted, unloved, disposable person like me couldn't feel comfortable in a place of sin where everyone was welcomed, where could I go?

The scariest part was that I knew it meant I would have to actually strive to become the man God would have me to be or die. But that meant work. It meant that I would have to leave the comfortable, familiar place of misery and pain that I knew so well. I knew from reading the bible, praying, and attending church, that God loved me and had created me fearfully and wonderfully. He wanted me to live an abundant life, which didn't include any of the things I was familiar with. All of my excuses were beginning to be swept off the table, but much like the Israelites being led out of Egypt by Moses, I was going kicking, screaming, complaining, and demanding to go back. Back to Egypt, back to slavery, back to misery and pain. So, I pasted a smile on my face and walked into the strip club. I wasn't ready to leave Egypt yet, even though I was now able to see it for what it was–a prison without walls. God was eagerly waiting to give me my miracle, but I wasn't ready for it yet.

Ben was waiting at a table with a big smile and a bottle of champagne. He quickly ordered two steak dinners, tipped the scantily clad waitress extravagantly and looked at me quizzically. "What's wrong man, you don't like champagne?" "I love it," I replied, "It's just that I'm really trying to stay sober, bro, I mean, I just got out of rehab like a week ago and you **just** got out..." I trailed off with a laugh. Ben scoffed and laughed arrogantly, "I was just there to get the judge of my back. He already took my license for a year, so I have to take cabs everywhere. Rehab just kept me outta the slammer, you know?" I nodded knowingly as our steaks arrived. Ben's attention went to his dinner and the strippers. I deduced that they had pegged him as a big spender because while most guys had to go up to the stage to tip them and get a little attention, there was a steady parade of strippers coming to our table. They were flirting with him, sitting on his lap, and getting tipped big time. I was pretty broke, and I guess Ben noticed, so he slid me 20 one-dollar bills so I wouldn't be too out of place.

I just couldn't get into it. It all just seemed so fake and forced. I was the only one who seemed to have a problem with it though. Everyone else was having the time of their lives. The men, the young women, even the bouncers were just laughing and dancing and partying. I sat there looking at my nasty, half-eaten steak trying to enjoy myself but having to admit it just wasn't my thing anymore. Finally, Ben was ready to go. "Hey, do you mind giving me a ride? I'm just over the Key Bridge in Rosslyn, (Virginia)." I knew it was only 10 minutes away, so I said, "No problem," and we left.

Once in the car, Ben got to what he really wanted. "Check this out, James, I need some crack, man. Do you know where to get some?" This is one of those moments I like to call a "Pop Quiz." This was a pass or fail situation; no in-between. How serious was I about my new life? I hesitated and he urged, "I'll make it worth your while, bro. C'mon man, please?" Now, I knew this guy had money. I saw lots of cash in the strip club and he had admitted to me that he had been a very successful contractor. Ben was so successful that he had saved up 5 million dollars, and his plan was to take a year off and a million dollars to live in hotels and party before returning to his business and 'normal' life. Greed got the best of me. I wanted a piece of that million. "Ok, man, I got you," I replied.

I drove him over to Northeast DC, saw a couple of guys hustling where I used to cop, and hopped out of the car. The two guys were obviously a dealer and a fiend who was working for him. They didn't know me, so I talked fast, "I know you don't know me from Adam, but I used to cop over here from Boobie and Black. I also know the dope fiend, Redz" they recognized all the names and their faces softened. "Look, man, straight up, I'm clean. I just got out of rehab, but while I was there, I met the white boy I got in the car. He just got out and he's trying to go." "How much?" the dealer asked. "$100," I replied. Their eyes widened and they both smiled, "Oh hell yeah, what your name is?" "J," I answered, "They call me J." "Ok, J, here you go I'm out here all the time. They call me Big Ant." "Ok Big Ant, that's a bet," and I was gone.

Back in the car, I handed Ben the rocks, "Here you go, man." He was excited. "You got it?! Oh, hell yes! Thank you, James!" I was thinking, "You can miss me with all the thanks and slide over the 'make it worth your while' cash!" But Ben wasn't thinking about me. He had a pipe and was lighting up right there in my car. He blew it out and said, "Yeah this is good! Hey, you want some?" I saw what his game was. Pay me off with a few hits of crack. But I was serious about not using. "No, man, I don't want any. I kinda thought I'd get some cash for putting my life and freedom on the line back there." That woke him up a bit, "Oh yeah, you're right. Here you go," he handed me $100. $100? I was just hoping for $20 at the most. Oh snap! This made it all worthwhile for me and started my new life as a middleman.

Chapter 15

The Middleman

Ben started calling me all the time, at all hours to pick up drugs for him. We established a pretty good system. If he wanted $100 worth, he would ask me to pick up a single-topping pizza. If he wanted $200, he would ask for a double. When I dropped it off to him, he always gave me $100, without fail, and I was dropping off 5-10 times a week. This doubled and tripled my weekly earnings. I started buying nice clothes for me and jewelry for my girlfriend. She knew what I was doing and didn't like it, but she never turned down a gift. I remember the first time I went to put gas in my car and just let it flow until it clicked without watching the amount. That was the moment I realized that money was not a worry anymore. Basically, I was a drug dealer, with only one customer, but he was a doozy.

This went on for a couple of months and then, predictably, I decided to try using again. I had a few thousand saved, a decent job, and everything was going well. What could a little using hurt? It hurt a lot. I'm an addict and it's a progressive disease. Very quickly, I was using more than ever. I only had to see my PO once a month at that point, so I had lots of days to get high and I did. Within a few weeks, I was fired from my job. Also, Ben could tell I was using, and he lost respect for me. He started paying me in drugs and only a little cash. I went from a clean, sharp-dressing dude to a crackhead/dope fiend in a matter of two or three weeks. It was scary how fast it happened.

After I lost my job, another dope fiend taught me a new hustle: stealing copper. He knew about an abandoned apartment complex on East Capitol St that was loaded with copper pipe. Since I had a car, he let me in on it. I couldn't believe how easy it was. We would go into the building and gather $150–$200 worth of copper in an hour or so. It was so sweet we started calling it our ATM. That lasted most of the summer of '06 until we started struggling to get enough to feed our habit. In the midst of all of this, my girl was still hanging in there with me, but was beginning to lose patience. I kept trying to quit on my own and I must've "kicked" the heroin habit half a dozen times. It would be two to three days of hell and then go back to it a week later. I just couldn't stay clean. It went from bad to worse as now even that once-a-month drug screen came up dirty. I had already used my last chance by going to rehab, so in October of 2006, my PO revoked my parole and sent the US Marshals to my house to take me back to jail.

"James? Where's James? Are you here?" I shook my head groggily as the voice wafted up the stairs. I was just waking up on a Sunday morning, on the second day of yet another attempt to kick the heroin habit. I wasn't as bad off as the day before, but I was still "ill" with no energy. I heard someone calling for me and my addict's brain thought it might be my buddy, Blue coming over to get me high. All the intentions of kicking went out the window as I scampered out of bed and threw open the bedroom door. "I'm right here," I began. My voice stopped short at the sight before me. Five huge United States Marshals were crowding up the small staircase heading right for me. "James LeBlanc?" the lead Marshal asked. I thought about running back into my room and out the second-floor window but realized that was foolish plus I didn't have the energy. "Yeah, that's me," I answered. "C'mon, bud, your PO revoked you. You gonna give us any trouble?" "Trouble?" I thought. What a joke. I wondered why they sent the entire Washington Redskins' offensive line to pick up a 160lb dope fiend. Five of the biggest guys I've ever seen to 'capture' me. I grinned wryly and put my hands behind my back to be handcuffed. Off to jail on a parole hit. My biggest regret was giving back three years of street time. I'd have to do that all over again whenever I got released.

Chapter 16

Surrounded by Chaos

Back in DC Jail, it was worse than ever. They were barely feeding us; I mean we were literally hungry. This is the first time in my life that I ate sugar sandwiches just to ward off the hunger. I was begging the trustees for extra food. It was also more dangerous as someone was always fighting. I stayed out of the way and prayed I'd survive until the parole board decided how long I would have to do on my violation. Finally, after about a month, I went before the board. They read my violation paperwork and dished out an eight-month hit. I would be in jail until June 2007 and then I would have to walk down the four years left on my sentence from the street. Originally, in 1999, with good time, I would have been done with my whole sentence in 2007, but now it would be 2011 before I could hope to be "off paper" and totally free. This was yet another sign of the insanity of addiction. It would take me twelve years to complete a three to nine-year sentence.

Once I learned my fate, I wondered if I would have to do the whole eight months in the hellhole of DC Jail or if I'd be shipped off to another location. My answer came about a week later. They loaded up two busses of DC inmates and shipped us off to Moshannon Valley Correctional Facility in Philipsburg, Pennsylvania. It was 200 miles and a four-hour bus ride away. As we drove through the Pennsylvania mountains, the guards told us the facility we were heading to was only 25 miles from Penn State University. "So close yet so far," I thought. They also told us that Moshannon Valley was actually a deportation center which was mostly used to house guys who were being sent back to their country. They were only taking some DC guys up there because DC Jail was so overcrowded. As we pulled up, we realized the full impact of what this meant–90% of the inmate population there was Latino, and they were upset about having to go back to their native country. Most were from Central America, places like El Salvador, Honduras, and Mexico. I looked at the angry faces watching us disembark and I looked at the defiant DC faces staring back at them and I thought, "Maybe this wasn't such a good idea."

The decision to send us up there made sense on paper. All the DC guys shipped to 'Mo Valley' were "short timers," meaning we were all doing two years or less. It seemed reasonable that guys with a little bit of time to serve would stay out of the way, be compliant, and go home. It seemed that way on paper. Unfortunately, the powers that be didn't factor in a very important component to the equation: Washington DC inmates. Washington DC is well-known in the prison system. Having been shipped all over the country when the feds took over, DC had to unite and fight or be run over. So, DC, or 'the homies' as we called each other, united. Even guys from beefing neighborhoods dropped the beef and came together in the name of DC, which was usually very effective because one thing DC is famous for in jail is the ability to fight. The problem at Mo Valley was that there were 1000 guys being deported and only 100 of us. 10:1 aren't good odds. I was all for staying out of the way, letting the Latinos run the place, and going home in June. Makes sense, right? Not to the DC guys. That didn't make sense at all and they were going to let it be known.

Things went ok for a few weeks, but then guys started to get "disrespected" here and there. Again, in jail, "disrespect" takes many forms and when you add cultural differences into the equation, the outcome is predictable. Tensions started to rise in the yard and talk in the dormitory-style pod started turning to war. I started hearing the recurring sound of "scrape, scrape, scrape," every night as I lay in my bunk. The young'uns were taking shifts sharpening shanks in the bathroom. I lay on my bunk shaking my head. "So, this is what it has come down to," I thought, "I'm going to die right here in the mountains of Pennsylvania." From the Berkeley Hills to a cold, anonymous death in a deportation center. It was surreal, but I couldn't deny it. Death was a very real possibility and there was nothing I could do about it.

One day we were in the gym working out and I noticed a couple of the MS-13 guys slip in and lean back on the wall watching us. "Nothing to worry about, just posturing," I thought. I looked up a couple of minutes later and I noticed another one had posted up. Hmmm, still no real problem. I did another set and looked up and I couldn't believe it. There had to be thirty of them on the wall. "How did they all...where did they all come from?" I quickly realized that the other ones had already been in there working out anonymously in ones and twos. The three who had slipped in were the leaders, who had signaled the others to mob up. We just looked at them. There were only about six or seven

DC guys in there and there was nothing we could do. The thought went through my mind again, "This is where I die." They just stared at us. Some were sneering, and some were shadowboxing, so we just waited for it to kick off. Suddenly about ten guards rushed in and made everyone go back to our housing units. I was relieved, but I knew now that it was just a matter of time. Their actions were blatant disrespect and we would have to retaliate.

"Alright ya'll know what time it is. We bout to go out there and handle these bammas!" Moe, one of the DC shot callers, was talking. It was two days later, and we were all huddled around him in the pod a few minutes before we went out to the yard for rec. "Now, we are all short timers, so we understand if you don't want to go! But I'm going and I know all the **real** soldiers are going out there cause we'd rather die fightin' than lay down and be disrespected!" The guys were getting all fired up, putting as many layers of clothing and whatever padding they could under their clothes in case they got shanked. I was standing there thinking that a little disrespect wasn't so bad. Let's just stay out of the way, do our little bit of time and go home. But I knew that wasn't the code in jail. You either fight or you get run over. If I took the "out" he had offered up and stayed in the pod while they went out to war, I'd be marked as a coward and probably beat up or stabbed when they got back. There was a group of four of us Christians in the pod and we had discussed what we would do amongst ourselves the night before. All of us except one decided to go to war with the homies. We didn't see any other way. The one guy was steadfast though, and he wasn't going. His position was that it was pointless to fight over respect in somebody's jail. He said he had prayed about it and God didn't want him to go, so he wasn't going.

Secretly, I admired him. He showed more courage than I did that day, because he stood up for what he believed in. I was just trying to survive.

Out we went that cold February afternoon. It had snowed the night before and there was snow and ice all around. We walked out into the yard, which was empty at that point, except for us. There weren't any guards around which seemed eerily strange. Here we were obviously in war-mode and no one seemed to mind. Were they just going to let it happen? Maybe they were keeping the Latinos inside as a safety precaution which made more sense. Just as I was getting my hopes up, the gate on the opposite side of the field opened, and the Latinos came walking towards our tiny group. They were spread out in a huge mob and we walked towards them in a line of twos. I was scared out of my mind and I was **way** in the back of the line. I watched as the leaders approached each other and started talking. "Ok," I thought, "Maybe they'll talk it out. Dang there's a lot of them! And where are the guards? Don't they see what's happening?" We kept walking closer and closer. I felt like I was in a dream. "This isn't really happening is it?" Suddenly, someone said the wrong thing and the leaders started throwing punches.

Shanks came out and it quickly became complete chaos. I started moving around, bouncing on my toes with my head on a swivel. Everything was happening in slow motion and I felt my senses sharpen to an incredible level. I squared off with a couple of guys, but we could look at each other and tell we were just out there. Our hearts weren't in it, so we'd drop our hands and move on. I kept bouncing around, ready to defend myself, but I was never targeted. The Latinos obviously knew who they wanted, and they concentrated their efforts on the leaders. Finally, Moe, the same guy who rallied us up in the pod, yelled, “It’s too many of them! Fall back!” “Thank you!” I thought. “You didn’t freaking realize there were too many of them before we came out here?” I was thinking to myself. We were all more than happy to ‘fall back,’ because **everyone** sprinted back towards the pod. I ran past blood in the snow and wondered who got dealt with. Unbeknownst to all of us, the pod door was locked when we tried to retreat. We frantically waved our hands at the camera trying to get the attention of the guards in the control bubble so they could pop the door. Nothing. In fact, there were **still** no guards in the yard! They clearly let it happen. Maybe they wanted to teach the DC guys a lesson? I didn’t know, but it was a cold-blooded move on their parts, nonetheless. The Latinos were packing rocks in snowballs and firing them at us. They started throwing trash cans at us as they got closer and closer. It looked like we were going to have to do some serious battle as they got right up on us, and then just as they pushed in for the attack, the door popped open.

We tumbled in and shut the door quickly. We could hear the Latinos pounding on the door and yelling at us. I looked at our motley crew in that hallway. Some guys had gotten pretty badly beaten. Some of their faces were covered with blood and I found out later that a couple of guys had gotten poked with shanks and some had broken ribs from being stomped. Meanwhile, I was untouched and looking fresh. Moe was walking around dapping people up and congratulating everyone on standing tall. When he got to me, he asked loudly, “Damn man you look way too fresh! Ay yo what was ‘J’ doing out there? Anybody see him?” I stood there speechless, knowing that I was screwed. I hadn’t done a thing and it was by the grace of God that I was unharmed. That didn’t matter to them, though. I was about to be marked as a sucker and a coward even though I had gone to war. Surprisingly, one of the young leaders, Tre, spoke up. "I saw 'J' out there. He was rumbling, man!" "Oh, ok," Moe said as he dapped me up. "Solid, man," and he moved on. I breathed a sigh of relief and nodded my gratitude to Tre who nodded back as he threw his shank in the trash.

After the riot, we were all shipped down to North Carolina. An eight-hour ride away, I finished my time there and it went by pretty easily. Everyone who had been in the riot was now marked as battle-tested and we were highly respected. Even though I didn't throw a punch and was untouched, I had been there and that was all that mattered. The guy who had stayed in the pod and didn't go to war with us was unharmed, but he was considered a coward and a sucker. He was my Christian brother though, so I didn't disown him like a lot of guys did. I knew he wasn't scared; he just wasn't going to fight for something he didn't believe in. In a way, I respected him for that.

As I neared my release date in June of 2007, I started doing a lot of reflecting. I knew that something had to change. Every time I jumped back into the druggie life, things became worse. What was going to happen next? I knew I was running out of chances and that death was becoming more and more of a possibility. My youthful invincibility was gone, and I knew it was only God who had carried me this far. Yet every time I got another chance, I threw it in His face and went back to my old ways. Why? Why couldn't I be happy? Why couldn't I have a normal, peaceful life with a house, a family, and a decent job? I was 38 years old and I was being released from jail to my room above the church. Back to the belly of the beast in the same neighborhood I just left. What chance did I have? I realized that although I knew He had carried me,

I was also very angry with God. "Why did you create me? Just to suffer? I was given away at birth, Dad left when I was seven, I was abused as a child, my brother was ripped away from me at 10, and I was given drugs at 12. What chance did I have? On top of all of that, you curse me with an addiction that I can't control unless I go to jail or rehab! Thanks, God! You must think this is really funny." I blamed him for everything. He could have made me differently, right? Why do I have to go through all this? No one else from Berkeley was winding up in prison riots in the mountains of Pennsylvania! Why me? Why am I so special? I felt so sorry for myself that all I could do was I cry myself to sleep those last few nights before my release. I knew what I was going to do when I got out and it wasn't going to be pretty.

Chapter 17

A Change is Going to Come

In June 2007, I was released back to my room over the church. I stayed clean for about a week, but temptation wasn't far away. By then, heroin was being sold right on my block. I had only to step foot outside and I could cop. Since I didn't like heroin without crack, I went and got that too and it was on. I managed to get my old job back by working for my old boss for a full weekend for free. I did well enough, so he hired me back. I was a star at the trap house that I frequented, because dope fiends really admire the ones who manage to get a job and hold it down. I did pretty good for a couple of months, only using when I had three to four full days before my next drug test. Soon enough I was back to operating in 'I-Don't-Care mode.' Addiction is a monster! Even knowing that I had **just** gotten out of jail, had **just** been in a prison riot, and had to complete close to four years of probation, my disease told me that none of that mattered. Let's go get high. I had proven during my years of incarceration that I didn't **need** to use, and I actually **liked** being sober, but I couldn't stop. The pull was just too strong. I also knew that God had delivered me from the bondage of addiction, but like the Israelites leaving Egypt, I preferred to stay in bondage. It was familiar to me. At least I knew what to expect and I could get some feel-good moments here and there, right? Being clean was too scary. Actually dealing with life, feelings, relationships, and responsibilities was too scary. I realized I didn't know how to live, so, full of self-pity and resentment, I continued to use.

I woke up ill one day but still managed to drag myself into my work truck and out to the first of my jobs for the day. I dragged myself around the projected dig area and spray-painted the sidewalk where I got readings for utilities. Red for power lines, orange for communication, blue for water, and yellow for gas. I put my instruments back in the truck and sat down heavily. A half hour down and 7 ½ hours to go. No way was I going to make it. But I was broke and owed my dealer money so I couldn't get any on credit. All I wanted to do was go home and curl up in my bed. So that's exactly what I did. I called my boss and told him I couldn't do the job anymore and to come get his truck. I went up to my room and crawled under the sheets. When I woke up and looked out of the window a few hours later, the truck was gone. Now I had no job and no money, plus I was ill.

I went back to the copper hustle for a month or so, but I couldn't believe how quickly I was going downhill. Before, I always had a little fight in me. A little something that invariably gave me hope, but now even that was gone. I knew I wasn't going to last long like this, and I was scared. One day, I used some drugs, and nothing happened; I couldn't even get high anymore. I felt like there was a dark cloud all around me and I was entering a very deep state of depression. I started pacing around my room cursing myself. "You idiot! You f***ing idiot! Look what you've done to your life!" I hated myself so much. I yelled and cursed and then I started punching myself in the face. I literally beat myself up, so much so that the next day my face was lumped up. When I got tired of that, I looked up towards the ceiling and started in on God. For ten solid minutes I cried, cussed, and yelled. I blamed God again for even letting me be born and for allowing me to suffer. I called God every name I could think of, in what I know now was an effort to get Him to kill me. I didn't have the nerve to take my own life, so I figured if I could anger God enough that He would do it. He didn't. He just let me get all of that bitter venom out of my system and then, surprisingly, I felt God's love enveloping me. I didn't want him to love me, because I knew I didn't deserve it. I wanted Him to kill me, but God was persistent. Who else but a loving God would allow his son to viciously cuss him out and then relentlessly cover His poor, tortured son in warmth and love? I felt God telling me, "I always knew you felt that way. You're finally being honest with me, Jim. I love you. Let me love you."

The gospel artist Donnie McClurkin sings a song called "So in Love," (2003) which is a love song from God to us. In it he sings, "When I found you you were all alone/ All of your strength and hope were gone/I gave you my heart to help you carry on/And then you turned and walked away/But I stayed right by your side/Many nights I sat with you and cried/Still you turned around and denied me/But I still stayed, I stayed." I didn't understand the depths of that song at the time, but that's what I felt that afternoon above the church. I knew that God had always been there from the very beginning. It was me who had done what I wanted to do. Even when I came to know him and experienced firsthand the showering of His love and the touch of His Spirit, I still turned and went my own way. The song continues, "Tell me what I did to you/To make you do me like you do/All I did was try to prove/Prove to you that I love you/Tell me what I have to give/In order for you to believe/Believe that I'll never leave/ Believe me when I say that I love you so." I fell to my knees and then to my face and sobbed. A body-wrenching ugly-faced, gasping sob. When I was done, I was tired, but it was a good tired. I called Pastor North and told her I was going to the detox center. Again.

I went to the detox facility on the grounds of the old Washington General Hospital right next to DC Jail. After I was detoxed, I asked to be sent to a long-term, faith-based rehab. I knew 30 days of rehab and then returning back to my neighborhood was not going to work. Actually, I was clear that I could never return to live in that neighborhood again. There were two programs available to the public–one was a one-year program and the other was 18 months. I knew I needed a lot of help, so I chose the 18-month program.

When Central Union Mission was founded in 1884, it was a homeless shelter which mostly housed civil war veterans who were struggling with alcoholism. Over the years, it expanded its scope to include an 18 month "Spiritual Transformation Program" (STP) which I joined in October of 2007. I stayed there until I left in May of 2009 and it was a life-altering experience.

Upon arrival, I was put on the 4th floor where the general population of about 100 homeless guys, slept on bunk beds in a huge room. The smells and sounds were tough to deal with, but it was explained that I had to stay here for a couple of weeks to prove I wanted to be there. Then, I would be moved to the third floor where the STP men slept. That floor was split into seven rooms with three to four men in each room, which seemed like a huge upgrade! While on the 4th floor, I was still expected to participate in all of the STP activities, which included: a prayer and devotional meeting in the morning after breakfast, a job around the Mission during the day, bible study classes every afternoon after lunch, and participation in the nightly worship service or bible studies that were conducted by outside ministers and churches after dinner.

It was a serious regimen and it got me used to a daily routine as I studied the bible and began to have a real relationship with God. After five months, I was sent to the second phase of the program, which was to spend three months at Camp Bennett in Olney, MD. It was almost like a spiritual retreat where we lived on a huge farm away from the hustle and bustle of Washington DC. There, we continued studying and did lots of farm work. Upon arrival back from the camp, I entered into the third phase and was ready to start working and/or going to school. I chose work and quickly got a job as a telemarketer.

Everything was fine until September of 2008 when, with 11 months clean, I decided to try drugs again. I had been talking to a young lady and we started seeing each other. I thought that we were becoming an item, but she didn't get that memo. When I discovered that I was the only one who thought we were in a relationship, I was hurt and disappointed. The old feelings of rejection and abandonment surfaced and off to the races I went. Remember the insanity of the addict's thinking of, "I'll show you, I'll hurt me?" Well, that's exactly what I did. I used for a few weeks and was discovered. The Mission staff sent me to another shelter for 30 days as punishment and then let me return. I returned in November, clean again and ready to give it another try.

As 2008 turned to 2009, I was feeling optimistic. Although I had had a relapse, the overall trajectory of my life, spiritually and physically was improving. I had joined a church in Laurel, MD and they sent the van down to the Mission on Sundays and Wednesdays to take us to services. I was back in touch with my family in California and they were hopeful. I got a job doing direct marketing in Home Depot and was actually making pretty good money. Since I had been at the Mission for well over a year at that point, I was becoming a leader in spite of the relapse. The Director of the Mission, Mr. Treadwell sat me down one day and told me I should go back to school, preferably bible college. He said he saw something in me and if I could stay clean and continue to develop in my spiritual walk, I could one day be an effective minister. Well, I truly respected Mr. T. and when he gave me that fatherly advice, I ran with it. I called Washington Bible College and began the process of registering for the Fall 2009 semester. Things were looking up again. I had people supporting me and even a church family behind me. I wasn't quite finished self-sabotaging, though.

By April of 2009, things were really progressing for me at work. I had had a great week booking appointments with Home Depot customers for free in-house consultations for cabinet refacing. For every appointment I booked, I received $40. That can really add up when you're booking 5-10 appointments per day. There was a huge bell at the office of the contractor which you rang every time you booked five or more appointments in a day. It seemed like I was ringing that bell every day. Things were going great, as I was saving money to go to school in the Fall. True to form, this was the perfect time to mess it all up.

You can be saved, sanctified, and filled with the Holy Ghost, but if you don't deal with your underlying issues, they will always haunt you. Instead of being transformed by the power of God, your religion will become a behavior modification program and those are usually temporary. I was doing fine on the outside; however, internally, at the depth of my spirit, I didn't believe that I deserved anything good. This is why an addict will sabotage success seemingly inexplicably. Usually, the causes and conditions can be traced back to resentments. Resentments, grudges, and unforgiveness will keep many, an otherwise, talented, intelligent person prisoner to the negative behavior that ruins their lives or keeps them from reaching their full potential. So, the miracle for me, was never in getting clean. I had successfully been able to get clean for long stretches of time when I was incarcerated, although I returned to using. The real miracle would come later.

One Friday evening in May of 2009 on the way home from work, I told my ride to pull over on North Capitol and H St NW. He looked concerned because it was not my normal hop-out spot, but I told him I was "going to go see this girl." He smiled, nodded, and pulled off, telling me he'd pick me up on Monday morning at the usual spot. I waved and ran to hop on the X-2 bus which took me to 17th and Benning Rd. NE. From there, it was a quick walk up to 17th and D NE where I could cop the crack and heroin I so badly wanted. I never met my ride to that job again. The disease of addiction is so progressive that I turned into a dope fiend almost immediately. I remained in that state for all of May and into June as I somehow evaded detection at the Mission and managed to land a job as a barista at Starbucks on 16th and New Hampshire Ave NW. Yet, I knew that I wasn't going to last at the Mission much longer. One Sunday morning, when none of the permanent staff was at the Mission, I called a woman I had been seeing casually to come pick me up along with my three trash bags of belongings. I snuck out of the Mission and moved in with her that very day.

"Miserable" is the only word that I can use to describe the five weeks I lived in a luxury apartment in Laurel, MD with a woman I didn't even like. After a few weeks, I believe she didn't like me much either, but boy did she try. She even let me use her car all day after I dropped her off at her job at a government agency in DC in the morning. I would go to my job at Starbucks then pick her up in the afternoon. If I had some money, I would go use and be late picking her up with some lame excuse. Finally, when I couldn't take it anymore, I returned to the Mission, tail between my legs asking to come back. They could tell that I was still actively using and since I had also snuck away without a word, they denied my request. I was so mad at them! One more resentment to add to my list. One more person or group that had given up on me. They gave me a referral to a "work-bed" shelter on Lincoln Rd NE and I was out the door.

The Emery House is a shelter for men who are employed and drug-free. It houses around 150 men in rooms that hold five to ten beds each. I knew they would drug test me, so I "kicked" on July 16, 2009. When I applied on July 20th, I was clean. I also had paystubs and a negative TB test, so I was allowed to move in. The woman I was staying with gladly helped pack my trash bags and broke all the speed limits down the Baltimore-Washington Parkway, across New York Avenue, and up Lincoln Rd to the shelter. I pulled my bags out of her car and before the last one hit the pavement; she was gone! I shook my head, "Was I that bad?" I mused as I lugged my bags inside. I was shown to my new home, which was a dormitory-style room with five other beds. During my first night there, one of my roommates, an older gentleman, informed me that half the guys living at the shelter didn't work. They did when they moved in, but they lost their jobs. He was one of them, but he was ok because he received a nice social security check every month. "By the way," he added, "Would you like to join me in the smoking of some crack?"

I looked at him in amazement as he held out his hand and showed me the pipe and some nice-sized rocks. I remembered the old saying in the drug game, "The first one is always free." That's how they get you going and soon you're spending all of your money. I looked at him and shook my head, "Naw, man I don't fool with it." I almost couldn't believe what I was saying, but somehow God gave me the strength to resist. I knew if I was discovered I would be kicked out and I **really** didn't have anywhere to go at that point. At the end of the day, I really wanted to be clean. Something had changed in me since the prison riot. Ever since 2007, I was on a trajectory towards sobriety and a good life. I just didn't know **how** to live clean or what it would take to remain clean, so I had some bumps along the way. But on that July evening in 2009 at the shelter, I knew I wasn't going to join the old man as he slipped into the bathroom to smoke crack. My resolve grew firmer every time he poked his head out the door 'geeking' wide-eyed and shifty-jawed. "Wow," I thought, "Is that what I look like?"

I knew the shelter was my last chance and I treated it as such. I was there for five months and I stayed clean the whole time. I was promoted at Starbucks to shift supervisor and I started going to school at Washington Bible College. I regularly stopped at the Mission and talked with Mr. Treadwell, who was still very supportive, as was the rest of the staff when they realized I was serious. I didn't have a car yet, so my daily routine was to get up at 4:15am, hop on the 90 bus to be at work by 5am, and open Starbucks. I would work until noon, hop on a 50 bus to Metro to take the train to New Carrolton, and another bus to school. After class, I reversed the entire process and ate dinner at the shelter, checked out the AA meeting that a DC legend, "Happy" Harold brought there every night, studied for bible college, took a shower, and went to bed. I would wake up in the morning and do it all over again the next day. On Wednesdays and Sundays, I met the church van to go out to Laurel for service, or on some Wednesdays, I took the hour-long bus ride out to Laurel for bible study. The routine was good for me and I was getting stronger. The shelter even cleaned out an old storage room for me and put a desk in it so I could study in peace. I was doing well in school and I even had some positive friends and some support going for me. I got a sponsor in AA and started doing some of the "step" work it takes to stay clean.

One evening in December of 2009, one of the counselors at the shelter called me into his office. "James," he began, "I've been watching you." I smiled and waited. "What is he getting at?" I wondered. "You never know who's watching and who they're connected to James, remember that." "I will," I answered, still wondering what he was getting at. "This is my night job. My main job is at a place called Samaritan Inns. It's a recovery program, but it also has SROs." I knew SROs were Single-Room Occupancies. Was he telling me that he had a place for me to live? A place that wasn't in a shelter or a big room with five other dudes in it? Don't play with me! "Well, I'd like to recommend you to them as an SRO renter. It's only $400 a month. Do you have first and last month's rent saved?" "**YES**! I mean, sorry, yes, I do Sir," I stammered. This was amazing! I had been saving, but the market rent in DC was so high that I had no idea when I'd be able to move out. Now, I was on the verge of moving into my own place. This definitely felt like a miracle, or, at least a major blessing.

I interviewed for the place and on Christmas Eve, I moved in. I woke up on Christmas Day in my own room. I looked around with tears in my eyes and just repeated, "Thank you, Lord," over and over again. The room was humble, but it was mine. I lived in a suite with five other men, but we all had our own rooms. There were two shared bathrooms, a kitchen and a small dining/living room. Each room was furnished with a twin bed, a desk, an entertainment cabinet for a TV and a small refrigerator. To me, it was a palace. I went over to Gary's condo that Christmas day and exchanged some gifts and ate with him, his friends, and family. To his credit, whenever I got clean, he never allowed drugs around. I went back home Christmas night and thanked God for another chance as I looked forward to the new year.

Chapter 18

Hope Springs Eternal

The next year, 2010, was a good year for me. I stayed sober for the whole year! I fell nicely into the groove of my busy routine and it was working out. Up early, I could walk from Samaritan Inns on 13th and Euclid NW to my job at Starbucks in about 15 minutes. Then, I would change clothes in the bathroom and take the busses and trains to school and back home. I was close to my AA sponsor, who I met one night when he led a meeting at the shelter. He was guiding me through the 12 steps, but I was taking my time. He also encouraged me to go to more meetings, but I only managed to get to one every week or two. Going to meetings was the final piece of admitting I needed other people and I wasn't ready to go all in with that. I had learned at any early age that it didn't pay to need anyone, love anyone, or to be vulnerable. My childhood was full of people leaving me, hurting me or both, so I tried my best to be an island. I knew both intellectually and, in my heart, that I actually **did** need people, I actually *did* need love and relationships with others, but at the end of the day, I was scared. I was scared to be left or be ripped away like my brother was when we were just kids.

I was scared that once it was discovered who I really was, behind the façade, I would be ridiculed and left. I was scared that if I reached out, I wouldn't be accepted. I was scared that I didn't measure up and I didn't want to be found out.

I kept everyone at arms-length. Even in my relationships, I would only let people get so close and if I felt things getting too serious, I would push away by starting an argument and storming out. I still had a lot of unresolved pain and anger that kept me from enjoying true relationships with others. Experiencing the joy, pain, victories, and sorrows of life, **with** other people and not just among them, was difficult for me. I was clean, though and life got a whole lot better. I was doing very well in school and my family was proud of me again.

I was very thankful when my family flew me out to the Bay Area for Christmas that year. It was a great visit! I stayed at my mom's house, the same one that I grew up in, and visited everyone else from there. My brother, Chris even came over and the three of us caught up over dinner the three nights I was there. I visited with my sister, Barbara and my dad and stepmom, as well as nieces and nephews. I marveled at how everything seemed to go fine when Jim wasn't getting high. My cousin, Dale, was living with my mom at the time and was a huge help to her as she was getting along in age and experiencing a lot of health issues. Mom smoked all her life, probably since she was 14 or so, and she never exercised. She had just turned 70 and she said herself that she was amazed she was still here! I was thankful that she got to see me sober. I had been clean for a year and a half straight and on a good trajectory for three and a half years. I was able to forgive the abuse and difficulties of my childhood for the most part. She was my mom and I really loved her. I didn't like some of the things that happened, but I knew she had done the best she could during a very difficult time. I was a real mama's boy and I could tell she was proud of me. And that meant the world to me.

I talked to my mom quite a bit during that visit. A linguist, she had become the world's foremost expert on the Salinan Indians, a California tribe that was in danger of losing their entire identity, language, and culture before my mom, Dr. Turner, began working with them back in the 1980's. All of my teenage years, she was buried in her work. She received her Doctorate degree the same year I graduated high school in 1987, and she never stopped working with them. She was so important to them that when she passed away, they came to her memorial and paid tribute in their traditional way, with drums and beautiful songs. I was very proud of my mom when I saw the impact she had made on an entire people.

We talked about her work and my biblical studies. Mom was a church secretary by then, but she was so intellectual that she had trouble believing in the "fairy tales" of the bible. I asked her to read the Book of Acts because that was the book I couldn't explain away when I challenged the veracity of Christianity. Archeological findings and original writings verify that a man named Jesus walked among us, he was crucified, buried in a tomb, and the body disappeared. That is undisputed. The bible states that he was then witnessed by over 500 people, walking around and eventually ascended to Heaven, which is a statement that can be argued but which I choose to believe. What can't be argued is that after all of that, his band of cowardly disciples, who had all fled, cursing and disowning him, (except John), when he went to the Cross, suddenly became the boldest of evangelists. History records that at least eight of them died a martyr's death while insisting to their last breath that Jesus was who he said he was–the Son of God who came to save mankind from the punishment of sin and give eternal life to all who believe in him as Lord and Savior. They **knew** that they were in for a terrible time under Roman rule, and that they would be beheaded, stoned, burned, crucified, imprisoned, and exiled. Yet, still, they persevered. Why? Mom didn't have an answer, so I suggested the Book of Acts.

Acts was written by one of those eye-witness disciples, 'Dr.' Luke, and he claimed that Jesus sent the Comforter, the Holy Spirit, to indwell Believers and give us the courage to speak truth to power. In chapter two, (Acts 2: 5, KJV) he explained that on the day of Pentecost, thousands of people from "every nation under heaven" came to believe and were filled with the Holy Spirit and spread the Gospel. In chapter nine, (Acts 9:3–19, KJV) he explained that a Christian killer named Saul had a personal encounter with Jesus, changed his name to Paul, and became a great evangelist, spreading the gospel all over the Roman empire and writing two thirds of what is now known as the New Testament, much of it on scraps of paper while chained up in prison. Why? What about my conversion and transformation? I still had a long way to go, and more struggles to come, but I wasn't the hopeless, homeless, criminal dope fiend I had been. Could my relationship with the Lord have anything to do with that? Could the Holy Spirit be compelling me to live a different, godly life? I don't know if Mom ever came all the way around, but she gave it some honest thought. A later conversation I had with her on her death bed gave me reassurance.

I flew back to DC satisfied and content. It had been a great visit with my entire family, and the last time I would see my mom before she passed away in October of 2011. I went back to Berkeley for her memorial and it was very emotional. I cried like a baby. Afterwards, the entire family met at the family house in the Berkeley Hills and ate, fellowshipped, and reminisced. It was a beautiful evening. We buried my mom's ashes under her apple tree in the backyard and I was honored when asked to say a prayer. Later, I thanked God for sobriety and for being available to share her passing and experience the aftermath with my family.

What a year 2011 would end up being. I left my job at Starbucks and started working for my AA Sponsor managing his cleaning service. I also volunteered for his nonprofit organization that assisted returning citizens, (ex-offenders), to reintegrate into society. To make ends meet, I did security work at a nightclub in the Adams Morgan section of the city. I was clean, doing well in school, participating in church, and then I met the women who would become my wife. In August of that year, I met Marchelle.

Marchelle says she knew I was her husband the first time she saw me. All I knew when I saw her was, "Wow!" Marchelle is a beautiful woman, but what set her apart was her spirituality. She's been walking with the Lord all of her life, so when she saw her husband in me, I knew it was God. We started talking and since we lived in different states, I got the chance to really get to know her without the physical stuff getting in the way. I realized quickly that she was my wife. We visited each other a few times and continued talking. I visited her and her two sons in Michigan for Thanksgiving of 2011 and met her family- Mom, Dad, seven brothers and sisters, and many nieces and nephews. Her dad is a pastor and a great man of God, and her mom is very wise and loving. When we returned to her house, I got on my knee and proposed. I apologized for not having a ring yet, but I would be honored to be her husband and to raise her boys as my own. She said "Yes!" **provided** I work on getting a ring on her finger, asap!

That was tough because I was pretty much broke at the time. I was working two jobs just to make ends meet and also volunteering with the reentry program, but I was committed. While in Michigan, I received an email from another volunteer, John, who was retired and did a lot of work in the community in DC. Some weeks earlier, John mentioned that he liked how I volunteered like I was getting paid and he vowed to help me find a decent job. In the email, he requested my resume because he knew the Executive Director of a large non-profit in DC that needed a job developer. The salary was $45,000 which was beyond my wildest dreams! I was barely covering my $400 rent and $150 car insurance for my old Honda Civic with 250,000 miles on it. I scoffed at the email and was ready to disregard it. Who would hire me? But Marchelle, already in wife-mode, gently encouraged me to send my resume. What could it hurt? I reluctantly did so, and on January 3, 2012, I was blessed to start my new career. I attributed it to my wife-to-be, because she believed in me when I didn't believe in myself. It took a couple of paychecks, but I quickly bought her the best ring that I could.

We were married on April 21, 2012 surrounded by our families who all flew into Maryland for the occasion. It was a beautiful outdoor ceremony on a perfectly sunny day. Amazingly, the forecast called for rain all day, but the sun shone brightly all the way until the last guest left the reception. Afterwards, the skies opened up and it poured! We decided to live in Maryland so Marchelle and the boys moved to the east coast. It was a huge sacrifice that she made for me, because I was starting a new career and had support around my sobriety in the area. It was a tough transition for all of us though. Suddenly we were a family living in a small three-bedroom apartment in Laurel. We had some growing pains but through prayer and perseverance it has worked out really well. I took a step backwards when we moved to Laurel, in a way, because I felt that I was all good. I was married, had a family, a good job, so I thought that I didn't need AA and all the things that had been working to get me where I was. Remember the insanity of Step 2? Here we go again. I decided that I could take it from here. I stopped talking to my sponsor, stopped going to meetings, stopped doing all the things that worked, and in July, with two and a half years clean, I relapsed.

The insanity of addiction. Unfortunately, it happens all the time to addicts everywhere- frustrating and befuddling themselves and their loved ones. Everything was going great, but I decided to sabotage it all once again because deep down, I **still** didn't believe I deserved it. Regardless of all the blessings and all the second chances, I was still damaged goods thrown away at birth and undeserving of anything good. Disposable.

July 13, 2012 was Friday the 13th. At the time, I was taking the commuter train from Laurel to DC and then traveling to different business meetings during the day via subway or bus. It was around noontime, that I found myself at the Metro Center walking across a platform, transferring from one train to another. Suddenly, I heard a very familiar voice. "J!! Ay, J!" I knew that rough, hoarse voice anywhere; it was Blue, the guy who had introduced me to the copper hustle. The same Blue that I used with every day for six months back in 2006. Now, even before I turned to acknowledge him, I had a decision to make. I knew that there would be no friendly hello, small talk, and go our separate ways once I turned. The best thing for me to do would be to ignore him and hop on a train. But that didn't happen.

They say you relapse in January but don't actually pick up until June. I hadn't been to a meeting since March and it was now July. I was newly married, suddenly a family man, and trying to succeed with a brand-new career. At the time I needed a support system the most, I turned away from it. Like a baby antelope who had strayed from the herd, I was ripe for the picking, and the enemy, like a roaring lion prowling to and fro to see who he can devour, spotted me and launched into attack. With no defenses in place I turned, I hate to admit, with relief and gratitude towards the voice I knew so well. We greeted each other with smiles, handshakes, and hugs. How in the world did we happen to be at the same metro station on the same platform at the same time? We didn't contemplate it too long. After a minute of pleasantries, we decided to go get high. Blue took me over to Southeast DC where we proceeded to drink wine, sniff dope, and smoke crack. All of my best intentions went out the window as I sought relief the way I knew best. It didn't matter that I had almost three years clean, and that God had blessed me with a beautiful family and a promising new career. I just wanted to get high. The strange thing was the more I did, the less high I felt. It seemed like I was getting more and more sober and I could clearly see that I was sabotaging it once again. I left Blue and took the Metro and the commuter train back to Laurel with drugs still in my pocket.

I arrived back in Laurel and got in my car for the short ride home from the MARC Train station. I decided to stop at the grocery store and get some food and some flowers for my wife in order to camouflage my afternoon activities. This led me to the Weis supermarket, where I just started buying stuff.

Just then, my wife called. She has always had what I refer to as a direct line to God and she can always sense when something is awry with anyone she loves so she was worried when she called. I assured her that I was ok, but something in my voice told her differently. "Okay," she said unconvincingly, and we hung up. I carried my groceries and flowers back to the car and sat there in the parking lot. The boys were visiting relatives in Alabama, so they weren't home. I wanted to use the rest of my drugs, but I knew I couldn't use at home, even though our sons were gone. Marchelle definitely wasn't going for that. I decided to go with the old wisdom that the best place to hide is in plain sight, so I sparked up right there in the car.

Suddenly, as I smoked and snorted, I became aware of a presence. This presence was unlike anything I had ever experienced, and it scared me. There was a palpable, almost physical, darkness present with me in my car that day. I know it sounds crazy, but it was as real as anything I have ever experienced and still gives me shivers to this day. I knew what the presence was, and I still believe to this day, that the presence of Death visited me in my car that evening. I could feel Death sitting beside me in an almost overwhelming, heavy darkness that filled the car. Death was sitting there calmly, menacingly, letting me feel his presence. I knew what Death was saying to me, "I'm next. You've been to prisons and institutions. I'm next. You've had enough chances, James. You keep playing with me, but I want you to know: I'm next." I was scared to the core. I have been jumped in alleys, I have witnessed shootings, I have been in a prison riot, but I have never been as scared as I was in my car that day. Never.

I jumped out of my car and threw the drugs in the trunk. When I got back in, the heaviness faded, and I drove home in a daze. I walked slowly up the stairs of our garden-style apartment and Marchelle met me at the door, coming outside and closing the door behind her. She looked up at me and I saw a pleading desperation in her eyes with firm resolve just behind it. "James, I'm a different kind of woman. I hear from God and I always know. Whatever you've been doing today, and I know its drugs, you can't do this again, ever. Not once. I will leave and you will grow old alone. We are meant to be, but if you sabotage us, you will grow old alone. Whatever you need to do, I will support you until my last breath, but this cannot happen ever again." I looked into my wife's eyes and saw love, hurt, pain, and resolve. I knew she meant it. She was not going to put herself or our sons through the insanity I was on the brink of putting them through. I'd had people give me a lot of lectures before, but hearing those words from the woman I love, the woman I had vowed before God to share the rest of my life with, seeing her resolve and knowing that she meant it; coupled with the experience with Death a few moments earlier did something to me. I seemed to snap out of my daze, "Oh my God I still have stuff in the car, I'll be right back." I drove off and threw all the drugs and paraphernalia away in a dumpster. Then I came right back. I apologized to my wife and I cried. I had come so close to the edge. If I had gone over, I may not have returned, but God saw fit to give me yet another chance. That was Friday, July 13th, 2012. I haven't found it necessary to take a drink or a drug since.

hapter 19

The Miracle

The thing about addicts is that even with all that happened that day: drinking and drugging and not getting high; my experience with Death; my wife's talk; if you don't do the work on the inside to address the underlying issues around why you always choose to hide from life, to avoid pain, to hurt oneself and those you love, you will use again. That's why I'm so grateful for the 12-step model. When I read the history of the original 12-step group, Alcoholics Anonymous, I knew it was divinely inspired. Within a week, I asked a local man to be my sponsor. I knew he was 28 years sober when we started working together, but what I didn't know was he is a trained counselor and a godly man.

My sponsor patiently and gently guided me through the 12 steps and that is when I experienced the miracle. It happened when we got to steps 8 and 9. In these steps, you make a list of all the people you have harmed, become willing to make amends to them all, and then go and make amends. The only exception to not making amends is when it will cause harm to them or others. These amends go for any and everything. I had to contact the collectors of all my outstanding bills and arrange payments. I wrote letters to people, made phone calls, and orchestrated face-to-face apologies. The key to it was always focusing solely on my "side of the street." I apologized for what I had done. Period. Not, "If it hurt you, I apologize," or "I only did what I did because **you** did...." No. I simply apologized for what I had done and left the rest up to God. During that process, there were two amends I made that would open the door for my miracle.

They say, "You have to forgive yourself." I always heard that but never really knew how to do it. My sponsor suggested I write a letter to myself. Not to grown-up James but to little Jimmy, the innocent five-year-old boy who still lives inside of me. He explained that inside all of us big, tough, men there is a little boy who has been hurt. A little boy who has been traumatized and whose innocence was smashed. This belief goes for women too. Inside every grown woman there is a little princess who yearns for the times before their innocence was taken. Little Jimmy had been hurt, abused, and traumatized, yet through all that, no one had treated him as badly as I did. I fed Little Jimmy poison every single day for years. I took Little Jimmy to scary, horrible places; no one else did that. So, I apologized, from the bottom of my heart to the little guy with the big afro and infectious smile. The little guy who was so thrilled with life until life squashed that optimism. I apologized to Little Jimmy and then I did something that made a huge impact: I promised **never** to treat him like that again. Never. I am so happy to say that I have been able to keep that promise one day at a time.

The second amends was the one I made to my birth mother. I thought my sponsor was crazy when he suggested I put her on my 8th step list. "I didn't do anything to that lady!" I protested. "Put her on there, James. If you want to stay sober, I suggest you put your mother on the list." He explained that it would be a spiritual exercise that wouldn't make much sense but was necessary. As I reluctantly wrote the letter to the mother I had never met, I realized he was right. I still had feelings of resentment. I still felt the emptiness of not knowing who I came from and I resented her for that. I knew that if I didn't deal with that, I would use again. The emptiness and pain would once again overwhelm me to the point that I would seek oblivion in the escape I knew so well. Death had already let me know he was waiting.

So, I wrote a letter to my mother. It wasn't all "my side of the street" either. When I was finished, we went to a quiet place and sat down and prayed. Then, I breathed and meditated and after a time, I pictured myself walking into a kitchen with two freshly baked pies cooling on the windowsill. A beautiful woman of around 65-70 years of age was standing there smiling with an expression that said, "I've been expecting you. Welcome. I love you." It was my mother. I walked in, sat down, and ate the slice of pie she served me. As if we both knew it was time, I began to ask all the tough questions I wanted to ask. "Mama, why didn't you keep me? How could you just give me away? Why didn't you give them a picture of you so I'd at least know who I came from, that I could look at and say, 'That's my mama.' Where are you? Who are you? Don't you know how I **feel**? Rejected. Given away. Cast out. Unwanted. Why didn't you want me, Mama? What did I do to you? I was a baby! I wasn't good enough? Why?" I broke down at that point and cried for a while; a good, final, cleansing cry. I felt relieved, then I lifted my head and continued.

Now that I was able to get that out of my system, I could complete the amends. I apologized for resenting her all of my life. I apologized for holding her to a standard that I couldn't even reach. I apologized for assuming she could have kept me. I apologized for assuming she didn't want me. I apologized for holding her captive to a resentment that she didn't deserve. I told her that she must be a pretty strong woman to carry me for nine months only to give me away for my own good. I thanked her for not aborting me, and for passing her strength and intelligence on to me. I told her that we all make mistakes but that she must be an extremely beautiful, strong, intelligent, giving person. I knew what the report from the adoption agency said: That she agonized over the decision and kept me until the last moment, weeping as she gave me away.

I had chosen to ignore that but now I was accepting and recognizing it. I was **choosing** to believe that what she did was done out of love. She carried me for nine months and delivered me healthy and happy. I thanked her for that. Then, I did something I had never done before in my life. I prayed for my mother. I prayed that God bless her, and that God keep her in his arms. I didn't even know if my mother was still alive, but I prayed that I could meet her one day. I took comfort in knowing that if she were no longer here on this earth, I would see her in heaven where all my questions would be answered. Finally, I told my mother that I loved her, and I forgave her. I released her from the grip of resentment and gave her to God. I asked Him to bless her and keep her until the day we meet again, either here or in the hereafter. With that, I let my mom off the hook, and The Miracle happened.

I never realized how much that resentment had controlled my life until I let it go. Did I still yearn to know her? Of course! Did I still pray for even just a photograph of her? Absolutely, but now I was **free**. Holding onto that resentment wouldn't allow anything positive to enter into my life. I was closed off. However, when I released the grudge, my face softened and my arms relaxed with palms open, ready to receive. Now I could finally let others into my life and be open to dealing with life on life's terms.. I was a human among humans walking this life out along with everyone else, only now with a zest for truly living. The Spirit of God could start to guide me now and I was ready. Ready for life. Ready for sobriety. Ready for marriage. Ready for fatherhood. Ready to receive the abundance of blessings that God has stored up for me!

I realized that my life had always been full of miracles. God had his hand on me the entire time, but I just kept kicking against his nudging. Every time he tried to gently guide me, I would buck like a bronco and go my own way. The results were always disastrous. Now that I was free, and free indeed, I was eager to discover what was in store. I felt like I was on the verge of something big.

Things really got cooking during my 5th year of sobriety. The old-timers say when you reach five years, you receive "walking around sense." Things were becoming clearer and clearer and I definitely settled into the married life, fatherhood, and my career. I received some promotions, we moved from an apartment to a townhouse and then to a beautiful single-family home. I became licensed and ordained as a minister and eventually received a bachelor's degree in Pastoral Leadership. My wife obtained her master's degree in Human Services specializing in Marriage & Family Counseling. In 2015, my wife and I even held our own church services for a year, as God led us to stretch our ministry efforts. As that season ended, we continued to preach the Word at various churches and ministered regularly at jails, rehabs, homeless shelters and transitional houses. All the while, I continued to pray for my mother and my entire birth family. I earnestly prayed that I would meet someone I was related to one day, or at least somehow see a picture of a relative. I knew it was a needle in the haystack, yet I kept it on my "bucket list."

In September of 2017, I was absently scrolling through my old Facebook messages when I stumbled upon a message that I had clearly missed. It was from August of 2009, and Judy, the woman who helps people find their birth families, had responded to a message that I sent her that day. Years earlier, she sent me a list of parents who had babies, on my birthday, at the hospital where I had been born. I reached out to her in 2009 asking for the list again, but not really expecting an answer. She answered me the **same day** asking for my email address. Somehow, I had missed it! I believe that God allowed me to overlook it then because I wasn't ready, and now I was. I responded to Judy's 2009 message in 2017 not expecting a reply. To my astonishment, she replied almost immediately. Judy responded with a list of maiden names of the mothers and last names of the fathers of all the children born on February 15, 1969 at the hospital in San Francisco where I was born. There were also names of the babies. I studied the list and landed on a set of names that made sense. The father's last name could be African American's and the mother's maiden name sounded Anglo. The baby's name was Johnathon. I told my wife that I thought that was me.

God really sent me an angel when he gave me Marchelle. She knew how important this was to me and although I was doing well, the pain I still felt and the emptiness of not knowing showed. I don't know too many women who would have dug into this search like my wife, but when she got ahold of this bit of information, she wouldn't let it go. For two weeks straight, I watched her research the names on that list. She collaborated with Judy some, but acted independently for the most part. A few times she asked me a question or two and I answered to the best of my ability, but all she really had was the non-identifying summary from the adoption agency and the list of parents and babies from Judy.

Marchelle was able to piece things together combining the two sources of information. We knew the ages and descriptions of my mother and her two siblings so when those didn't match, she knew it wasn't my mom. She got to the name I had chosen and started to drill down. Reaching a dead-end, she was stymied for a day or so before coming up with an idea. Marchelle looked up the California Birth Index for the year we thought that my mother was born, based on the agency's report. Amazingly, there was only **one** baby girl born in California that year with that last name. Tracing the family, Marchelle came across the obituary for the baby's mother, (my "grandmother") written decades later. The obituary featured the names and ages for all of her children, and it matched exactly with the information we had from the adoption agency. The woman Marchelle thought was my mother was the eldest child and she had two younger siblings, whose ages and physical characteristics matched the information we had.

Marchelle quickly went to Facebook and looked them up. The younger sister even had red hair which was one of the characteristics matching the adoption agency's information. Bingo. This was it! My wife screamed for me to come upstairs. "Honey!!! This is your mother. I mean I really think this is your mom." She turned her phone towards me, and I looked at the beautiful, kind face smiling into the camera. Could it be? Could this be her? I dared not get my hopes up.

"Wow," was all I could muster up. "So, you think that's her, huh?" "Yes, honey. It **has** to be her!" she responded. "She is the **only** woman born in California in 1943 with that last name! Her brother's and sister's ages match the info we have. Honey, just **look** at her!" I had to admit...the eyes; it was in the eyes. "Wow," I whispered, "I mean, what if that's my mom, honey? Wow!"

We immediately called Judy with the news. She was amazed we had gotten that far and encouraged Marchelle to think about doing this for a living. My wife somehow tracked down a phone number so Judy said she would reach out to my "possible mother." She would tell her that she was a genealogist who was working with a gentleman who was tracing the family name and thought he might be related to her. Judy placed the call at the beginning of October and left a voicemail. As we waited for a response, we stalked my "possible mom" on Facebook. She seemed very, very nice, and she showed a genuine concern about equality and social justice. We clearly shared some of the same beliefs and worldviews. I started **really** hoping she was my mom. Could it be her? After 48 years of wondering, hoping, giving up, and hoping again, could it be? Meanwhile Marchelle had tracked down my father, or so she thought. From the agency's report, we knew his age and that he was possibly from Washington DC. She tracked down a man with the last name that was coupled with my 'moms' and he checked all the boxes. When she pulled up a picture of "Henny" I almost fell down. He was bald too and we had the exact same head shape, I mean **exact**. Somehow, I knew he was definitely my dad. Unfortunately, he had passed away in 2007.

Marchelle also tracked down a man she thought was my brother on my father's side. Again, looking at his picture on

Facebook, there was an uncanny resemblance. The feeling of being almost 100% sure that I was looking at a black man to whom I was blood related, began to fill my soul. I was on the verge of a fulfillment that I had previously thought impossible.

A month passed by and my "possible mom" was not responding. Marchelle was going to contact her directly, but Judy asked for one more chance. This time her approach was much more direct. She called her and told her very directly that this gentleman **really** thought he was related to her. This time the light bulb went on and she knew–her son. The son she thought about every single day for 48 years and wondered how his life had been. Is he alive? Is he happy? Does he think about me? Judy asked if it would be ok if I called her the next day and she told her "Yes, of course, that would be fine. I would love to speak with him." Her son.

Judy emailed me the next day with the news. I read it in my cubicle at work and lifted my eyes to Heaven. "Thank you, Jesus, thank you Jesus, thank you Jesus." I left the office and walked outside to the parking lot and called my mother. She was no longer my "possible mother" she was my mother. We spoke for the very first time on November 16, 2017- 48 years, 9 months, and 1 day from the day she gave birth to me. The conversation was surreal, and surprisingly easy. As we ended, we both said, "I love you." It was natural, unforced, and true. I hung up and said out loud, "I just talked to my mommy!"

I came home from work that evening to another surprise. "Honey don't be mad," my wife began. "Uh-oh," I thought. She continued, "I called your brother in Milwaukee, you know the one on your dad's side. I saw that he worked at a certain company, so I just called and asked for him. They transferred me and I was just going to leave a voicemail, but he picked up!" She went on to tell me that their conversation was halting at first and he wasn't convinced. He was trying to process this bombshell, but when he looked me up on Facebook while they were talking, his whole demeanor changed. He couldn't deny it. We didn't need to take a DNA test because the head said it all. "And by the way, him and his wife are calling tonight!"

Before my brother and his wife called, Marchelle and I called my mom so they could talk too. My mom thanked Marchelle profusely and proceeded to be open to anything we wanted to ask. "How did you meet my dad? What was he like?" I peppered her with questions, and that's when she confirmed that Marchelle was right. "Well," she began, "Henny, I mean Robert, sorry, everyone called him Henny, anyway, we met when I lived in Washington DC." Marchelle and I looked at each other wide-eyed and Marchelle literally fell off the loveseat! She had just used both the first name **and** the nickname of the man we suspected was my dad. This was final confirmation. Marchelle had been right all along, she really had found my family! I **finally** knew who I came from. I felt a sudden sensation of being completely filled up. My faith, the 12 steps, and my new family had done some 'filling,' yet it was this that filled the hollow space in my life. I suddenly felt that I had substance, and that I actually came from two human beings and now I knew who they were. It was truly an indescribable feeling. I thought I could never get clean- it happened. I thought I would never have a family- it happened. I thought I could never forgive my mom for giving me away- it happened. Now, this. I thought I would **never** find my birth family- it was happening as we spoke. We were speaking to **my mother** and later that evening we spoke to **my brother** who rejoiced with me about it all. Wow!

I was conceived in DC, and my first cross-country trip wasn't in 1991 after all. It was in 1968 in my mother's belly. Funny how I had wandered back to my roots. I looked heaven-ward again with a wry smile. "God, you've had your hand in this the whole time, huh?" I felt him smile and nod and give me a long, warm hug.

I hugged my mother for the first time on January 25, 2018. In Ephesians 3:20 (KJV), Paul writes that God is able to do, "...exceedingly abundantly above all that we ask or think, according to the power that worketh in us." I had only asked God for a picture, but he did "exceedingly abundantly above," and flew my mom into BWI Airport! We hugged by the baggage claim with Marchelle recording the entire experience. She is such a sweet, kind woman and I call her "Mommy," in honor of the little boy who is still inside me who always yearned to know his mommy.

During that visit, we drove down to Virginia and met my mother's sister, my aunt. Since then I have been to Mom's home in Idaho twice. There I met my brother, sister, niece and great-nephew. We have a family cabin in the mountains of Idaho and during my last visit, I met my mother's brother, my uncle, and his wife, my aunt. I have cousins, nieces, and nephews on my mom's side that I have yet to meet, but through the magic of Facebook, we talk virtually and are getting to know each other. What a blessing the acceptance I have experienced has been!

I actually met my brother on my father's side first. He and his wife flew into DC in December of 2017, and we met at the National Museum of African American History and Art. What an amazing feeling to walk through that museum with my African American family- my wife and sons, along with my brother and his wife. I felt like I had come home.

The 'filling in' process continued, and I felt more and more whole and complete. We met my elder sister that day and had lunch at her home in the Shaw neighborhood of Washington DC. There, they gave me my father's flag which, because he had been in the United States Air Force had been presented to the family at his funeral. What an honor and blessing to be entrusted with this heirloom. It is displayed proudly in my office at home. My brother also gave me my father's favorite cardigan sweater which I hold sometimes during quiet moments.

I had the honor of meeting two of my father's brothers before they passed away. The acceptance, love and wisdom my Uncle Lou gave me before he passed was priceless. I have many, many cousins in the DC area, one of which is a well-known pastor. The stories they have shared with me about my father have filled me with joy. He was everyone's favorite, sort of everyone's dad. He was the life of the party and a born leader. He lived on the wild side for a time, during which he met my mom, but he came to know Christ sometime in the 70's or 80's and never looked back. I am proud to be Henny's son. Back in 1968, my mom actually had to visit him in the prison at Lorton, (I followed in his footsteps in many ways), to tell him that she was pregnant. It was there that she found out he was married and had children. He wanted to try to figure it out and somehow keep me, but deeply hurt, she fled back to California where I was born in San Francisco. She already had one child, my brother who is three years older than me, and she was struggling mightily. Knowing that she wouldn't have much family support, with her father's deep Texas roots entrenched in racist beliefs, she made the heart wrenching decision to give me up for adoption. It was a chance at a better life. I **finally** knew the backstory, and as messy as it was, it made sense. Life happens, and it isn't always neat and pretty.

I couldn't have asked for a better outcome. I know that many adoption reunions do not end well, but I have been richly blessed by this experience. It is very unique meeting people who are strangers, yet the love I feel for them is instant and automatic. I was taken by surprise with how easy it was to have those feelings. Yes, it is surreal at times and we are getting to know each other, but the love was there at once. Perhaps it has always been there, in our spirits, just waiting for us to finally meet in person.

After meeting my family, I realized that my life would've been about the same. I still would have been a mixed kid with a white mom and a white brother and sister. So, at the end of the day, things worked out the way they were supposed to. I got to grow up in a fabulous neighborhood in a beautiful town. Yes, inside the house it was crazy, but I am grateful for the advantages I was exposed to growing up in the Berkeley Hills. Unforgiveness, emptiness, and addiction took me from there to the streets of Washington DC and even to a prison riot in the mountains of Pennsylvania; but through it all, God has had his hand on me. I have been in the gutter and locked up in a cage, but I have also experienced God's miracles. The miracle of sobriety, the miracle of finding my birth family, and the miracle that opened the door for it all- the Miracle of Forgiveness. I pray that you, too, can experience this miracle because it unlocks the door to a new life. A life where joy is everlasting, and miracles never cease!

Me as a baby with my sister Barbara, brother Chris and Mom.

Me with Dad and my brother and sister.

Jimmy

My oldest friend, Dan and I at a Warriors game, 2019.

My family: Marchelle, Marcus, Joshua and me.

Me and my mom during her first visit.

My dad, Henny.

Me, my mom and my
Aunt Marilyn!

My brother Rob and I- the first
time we met.

My brother Tony and I – Mom
took this the moment we met.

Me, Rob, my cousin Keith,
Marchelle and Marcus- trying
out for Family Feud 2019

Me, my niece Khloe and my sister Lori during my second visit to Idaho

Berkeley Family: My nephew Malcolm, niece Sylvia, step-mom Judy, me, Barbara, Chris, and Dad

Tony, my uncle Tom and me- going to cut down a tree at the family cabin.

With Marchelle's family after preaching at her dad's church- Easter Sunday 2019

James and Marchelle

Acknowledgements

My lovely bride, Marchelle. I love you!

Our sons, Joshua and Marcus you are God's blessing to us.

My gratitude to my dad and stepmom Dick and Judy LeBlanc; my sister Barbara,

my brother Chris, and posthumously, my mom, Dr. Katherine Turner. Thank you all for always being there and loving me!

My biological family: My beautiful mommy, Sharon Wander; posthumously my dad, Robert "Henny" Dodds; My brothers Tony, Rob, and Chris; My sisters Robin and Lori; All of my cousins, nieces, and nephews. A very special thank you to my cousin, Pastor Keith Battle for believing in this project and giving me guidance. Thank you all. The hole was filled when you entered my life!

The Fannings and The Marshes–Thank you for being family! My editor Dr. Ayesha McArthur: Thank you! There's no way this gets done without you. My coach, "Simply" Kashonna Holland, thank you for dreaming big with me! To Courtney and Patricia Stewart- you believed in me when it wasn't popular to! Jim and Jane Ennis- You know the real deal. Thank you. Daniel Fishlow- My day one. Who would've guessed back at Hillside!

To all the Friends of Bill across the world: Keep coming back, we need you. Everyone I haven't mentioned: Thank you for being a part of my journey and for having an impact on me!

The Lord Jesus Christ: Thank you, thank you, thank you. I love you and I'll see you when I get home.

References

McClurkin, D. (2003). So in Love. On ...*again* [CD] US: Zomba Recording LLC.